DARWIN

A BEGINNER'S GUIDE

GILL HANDS

Hodder & Stoughton

A MEMBER OF THE HODDER HEADLINE GROUP

Orders: please contact Bookpoint Ltd, 78 Milton Park, Abingdon, Oxon OX14 4TD. Telephone: (44) 01235 400414, Fax: (44) 01235 400454. Lines are open from 9.00–6.00, Monday to Saturday, with a 24-hour message answering service. Email address: orders@bookpoint.co.uk

British Library Cataloguing in Publication Data
A catalogue record for this title is available from The British Library

ISBN 0 340 790431

First published 2001
Impression number   10 9 8 7 6 5 4 3 2 1
Year   2005 2004 2003 2002 2001

Typeset by Transet Limited, Coventry, England.
Printed in Great Britain for Hodder & Stoughton Educational, a division of Hodder Headline Plc, 338 Euston Road, London NW1 3BH by Cox & Wyman, Reading, Berks

CONTENTS

CHAPTER 1: WHO WAS DARWIN?   1
Darwin's early life and times   1
Early education   3
University studies – Edinburgh   6
University life – Cambridge   8
Summary   12

CHAPTER 2: THE VOYAGE OF *THE BEAGLE*   13
Preparation for the voyage   14
The voyage begins   15
Across the Atlantic to Brazil   17
The east coast of South America, Tierra del Fuego and the
Falkland islands   18
The west coast of South America and the Galapagos   20
Australia and home   23
Summary   24

CHAPTER 3: TOWARDS A THEORY OF EVOLUTION   25
Evolution before Darwin   26
Evolutionary thinkers   28
Marriage and country life   32
Summary   34

CHAPTER 4: DARWIN'S THEORY OF EVOLUTION   35
Natural selection   36
Evidence and observation at home   39
Evidence from *The Beagle*   41
Fossil evidence   44
Geological theories   44
Biological observations   45
Summary   46

CHAPTER 5: THE *ORIGIN OF SPECIES*   47
The influence of Wallace   47
A brief outline of the book   49
Public outrage   52
Scientific debate   54
Darwin's supporters   57
Public acceptance   58
Summary   59

CHAPTER 6: DARWIN'S LATER YEARS   60
A busy life   61
Publications after the *Origin of Species*   63
The final years   70
Summary   71

CHAPTER 7: BEYOND DARWIN   72
Social Darwinism   72
Neo-Darwinsim   73
The birth of genetics   75
Mutations or Steady State?   77
Religion against science   78
Summary   80

GLOSSARY   81

CHRONOLOGY OF MAJOR EVENTS IN DARWIN'S LIFE   84

FURTHER READING   85

INDEX   87

Who was Darwin?

Charles Darwin is one of the most well-known scientists of the 19th century, his theories are still important and even today the subject of continuing debate. He is chiefly remembered for his theory of **natural selection**, a way of explaining the **evolution** of living things. He was not the first person to write about evolution. His grandfather, Erasmus Darwin, had published a book on the subject in 1796. Charles Darwin always said he was not influenced by his grandfather's ideas, and their concepts of evolution were quite different, but he was obviously more open to the idea of evolution than many of his contemporaries because of this family connection.

KEYWORDS

Natural selection, theory that natural processes cause the survival of living things best suited to their environment.

Evolution, development of species from earlier forms.

Industrial Revolution, period of history when trade and industry progressed rapidly due to technological progress.

The publication of his theories in Victorian England caused much controversy, for they seemed to challenge the foundations of Christianity. Today there are still people with strong religious beliefs who view Darwin as a mistaken and dangerous man.

DARWIN'S EARLY LIFE AND TIMES

Charles Robert Darwin was born on 12 February 1809, in Shrewsbury, England. When he was born Britain was going through a prolonged period of industrial and social change. The **Industrial Revolution** is generally believed to have started around 1750, but it gathered pace at the beginning of the 19th century and Britain began to be transformed from an agricultural society into an industrial one. Changes in society were reflected in the philosophy of the times. In the 18th century the 'age of reason' had led some philosophers to question the predominantly Christian view of the world. Continuing scientific progress led some thinkers to question the existence of God, although the majority of western Europeans were still largely Christian. Darwin's theories added fuel to this debate causing an uproar in the well-ordered society that is difficult to understand in today's more tolerant and religiously diverse world.

Darwin's mother Susannah was the daughter of Josiah Wedgwood, the founder of the famous pottery works, near Stoke on Trent, in England. The Wedgwood family was wealthy, partly due to its exploitation of new scientific methods for producing pottery. They were

KEYWORD

Unitarians, believers in a form of Christianity that sees God as an individual and not a trinity.

devout **Unitarians**, and Charles was brought up to follow this religion by his mother and sisters. These strong Christian beliefs probably contributed to the delay in the publication of his theories of evolution later in his life.

The Darwin family, too, was wealthy: Charles's father, Robert, was a well respected doctor and surgeon in the Shrewsbury area. He was a tall and imposing man, and although he loved his children and provided for them financially, he was often stern and domineering at home. With his patients he was gentle and was known for his excellent bedside manner.

Charles was the second son in a family of six siblings. Above him were Marianne, Caroline, Susan and Erasmus. The baby of the family was Catherine, who was 15 months younger than Charles. Although the Darwin children loved and respected their father and wished to please him, they also felt life at home was rather oppressive. This was especially true after his wife Susannah died in 1817, when Charles was only eight years old.

Susannah suffered from a tumour and during the worst of her illness Charles and the younger children were not allowed to see their mother; only Marianne and Caroline, who acted as nurses, were allowed into her room. In his autobiography he writes that he could remember little of her apart from a worktable that was kept in her sick room and a black velvet gown she wore. After the funeral she was never mentioned again.

The older sisters ran the household between them and Charles and Erasmus formed a strong bond against these teenage rulers. Caroline had been responsible for Charles's early education and was rather strict, although he confesses in his autobiography that one of his earliest memories was of trying to break windows in a room where he had been sent as a punishment, so perhaps he needed a firm hand.

Charles was four years younger than Erasmus, so as a small boy he often played alone in the countryside. His favourite pastimes were observing the natural world around him and fishing. 'The Mount', where he lived, was a beautiful, secluded house with a greenhouse full of exotic plants and gardens containing fruit trees and rare shrubs. The wooded grounds led down to the River Severn, which had excellent fishing.

He also enjoyed collecting things. In the way of young children he collected objects haphazardly, with no attempt at categorising them, an eclectic mix of postal franks, shells, birds' eggs and minerals. But it is in these hobbies that we can see the emerging interests of the older Darwin, who was, after all, a great observer and categoriser.

EARLY EDUCATION

At first Charles was educated at home by his mother and Caroline, but when he was eight he was sent to the Reverend Case's Unitarian day school in Shrewsbury. He did not fit in there at first, being a rather solitary little boy, and in a desire to get attention he began telling elaborate stories. These unlikely tales of natural history involved fantastical birds and the ability to change the colour of flowers.

In 1818 he was sent to join his brother at Shrewsbury School, a minor public school, not far from The Mount. Charles and Erasmus were both boarders here, but they often visited home during term time to see their father and sisters.

'School, ... to me, was simply a blank', he wrote in his autobiography. He found the traditional education of classics, mathematics and poetry extremely boring. He was fairly hopeless at both Greek and Latin and was not fond of games either. Lessons were usually learned by rote and recited in front of the class. When poetic compositions were required Charles and his classmates would find lines from old obscure poems in books and copy them out, pretending they were their own work.

In his teenage years Charles became less reserved and had many friends. He started riding in the hills with his brother and his Wedgwood cousins and began to enjoy the sport of hunting. He was still interested in collecting things, especially beetles and moths and minerals, only now he was able to identify and categorise his finds. Collecting was a fashionable pastime and most gentlemen had cabinets of curios on display.

His interest in observing the natural world was still strong; after reading the Reverend Gilbert White's *Natural History and Antiquities of Selborne* he became more interested in bird watching and wondered why all gentlemen did not become ornithologists.

He loved to read of far away places and enjoyed the Reverend C.C. Clarke's *Wonders of the World* which fired his imagination with tales of exotic foreign lands. At the time he dreamed of world travel, never believing those dreams would come true. He also enjoyed the works of Shakespeare and the odes of Horace and was often found curled up reading in the deep stone window ledges of the school.

His chief passion at the time was chemistry and Erasmus set up a laboratory in the garden shed after being banished from the house for making a mess. He made Charles his lab assistant and together they spent many happy hours in the school holidays mixing chemicals and making noxious smells. His friends at school heard of this and gave him the nickname 'Gas'. Dr Butler, the head of the school, did not approve of this activity at all, calling Charles a *poco curante*, someone who trifles in things. As Charles was such a poor scholar of ancient languages he had no idea of what the Doctor meant and felt it a 'fearful reproach'. In his autobiography he states that these early experiments in chemistry were the best parts of his education, 'for it showed me practically the meaning of experimental science'. The headmaster, however, believed the sciences to be 'useless subjects'. When Erasmus left school to attend Cambridge University, Charles kept on experimenting and wrote to his brother frequently about his finds.

The Darwin boys experimenting.

None of this enthusiasm, however, was channelled into his schoolwork and he was, at best an average pupil. His father despaired, saying: 'You care for nothing but shooting, dogs and rat-catching, and you will be a disgrace to the whole family.' He wisely decided that as Charles was making little progress in school that he should leave early, to follow in the family tradition and become a doctor or surgeon. Charles was not particularly keen, but always did his father's bidding – probably also thinking that anything would be an improvement on the boredom of school!

On leaving school Charles spent the summer of 1825 practising medicine around Shrewsbury, visiting his father's poor patients, mainly women and children, and making notes on their symptoms. Later he discussed these with his father who made up suitable prescriptions. He quite enjoyed this work, but he did not enjoy his brother's letters about his experiences in the dissecting rooms and the smell of the anatomy theatre. His family knew he was rather squeamish, he even killed worms in salted water before he went fishing, so that they would not be impaled on the hooks while still alive. He also hated the sight of blood, but it did not stop him from shooting things, so his father believed he would get used to the gory side of medicine eventually, as all doctors have to.

UNIVERSITY STUDIES – EDINBURGH

In the October of 1825 Charles and Erasmus started studying at Edinburgh University in Scotland. This was seen as one of the best medical schools in the world and Robert Darwin had some influence there with old friends and colleagues. Erasmus transferred from Cambridge to do his external hospital study and to keep an eye on his younger brother. They took lodgings together a few minutes walk from the university and soon settled into student life. The Darwin brothers found Edinburgh to be a cosmopolitan place after living in the countryside and they enjoyed the theatres and parties. It didn't stop them from studying, however, and they borrowed more books from the library than any other students in their first term.

Charles soon found that medicine was not for him. Operations at that time were extremely barbaric, being practised without anaesthetic. The patients were tied down, screaming, to the operating table, and the best surgeons were those who could hack off limbs in the fastest time possible. After witnessing a distressing operation on a child, Charles had to run out of the room and vowed never to attend again. His anatomy lecturer also disgusted him with his filthy appearance and indifferent manner. He found all his lectures tedious, except for those on chemistry given by Professor Thomas Hope. His main solace came through his hobbies: he visited the Scottish coast to collect marine specimens and he continued to hunt whenever possible. He decided to learn how to stuff animals from a 'blackamoor', John Edmonstone, a freed slave, from Guiana in South America. His master, a fine taxidermist, had passed on his skills. Charles found him interesting, 'very pleasant and intelligent' and he loved to sit and listen to tales of the rainforest and the animals that were to be seen there. This ability to preserve animal specimens was very useful in later years when Charles travelled on *The Beagle*.

KEYWORDS

The Beagle, survey ship that Darwin joined on a round-the-world voyage.

Radical, a person who wants fundamental change in political systems and society.

Materialist, one who believes that all ideas and beliefs are a result of the material world and not the result of divine intervention.

Erasmus went to London to study anatomy and Charles was left to study alone for his second year. He became increasingly disillusioned with his studies and spent more time on his hobbies. He joined the Plinian Society, this was a natural history society, where academic papers were read, but as many members were **radical** young students, debate often became heated. Many of them believed that the scientific world should be freed from superstitious beliefs and be divorced from religion. They subscribed to the **materialist** view of the world developed from the ideas of philosophers such as John Locke (1632–1704). This caused arguments with those who held more traditional religious views. When one of the members put forward a paper proposing that the mind and consciousness were not spiritual but were a scientific result of brain activity it caused a furore and the report on it was later struck from the records. This may have had some effect on Charles's view on publishing controversial work in his later years.

He gained many friends from the society and spent a lot of time with Robert Grant, an Edinburgh doctor with 12 years' experience who had given up his practice to study marine life. He was a great believer in the works of the French evolutionary thinker, Jean Baptiste Lamarck, and had read Erasmus Darwin's work on evolution, *Zoonomia*. He discussed these beliefs with Charles as they went walking together on the coast, observing sea slugs and sponges.

Charles also enjoyed geology, attending lectures by Robert Jameson. The lectures were rather dull but Jameson ran a museum in Edinburgh where Charles spent a lot of his spare time, happily stuffing birds. However, this was not the reason for his studies in Edinburgh and he spent little time and interest on his medical career. The fact that his family were rich gave him little incentive to struggle with a subject that he hated, for he knew he would never have to earn his own living. He left Edinburgh in April 1827 with no qualifications, but with a great deal of experience and knowledge that would come to shape his future theories.

UNIVERSITY LIFE – CAMBRIDGE
When Charles left Edinburgh he travelled for some months, visiting Paris, where he met up with some of his Wedgwood cousins. He enjoyed the shooting season both at Maer, the Wedgwood family home, and in Shropshire. It was at home that he became romantically involved with a local squire's daughter, Fanny Owen. Fanny loved to hunt and play billiards with the men and was something of a tomboy.

Robert Darwin worried about his reckless son, he seemed to be wasting his time and his money, drifting aimlessly about with no thought for the future. He decided that Charles should become a minister in the Anglican Church, although he had been brought up as a Unitarian. The Church of England at that time sold rural livings to those who could afford them and Robert Darwin had plenty of money. Country parsons were known to enjoy hunting and mixing with the middle and upper classes.

Charles was not totally convinced by this plan, since, although he did believe in God, he was not deeply religious. However, he could see no other way forward, especially as his father was supplying him with money. He thought he would probably enjoy the life of a country parson if it gave him a chance to emulate the Reverend White and spend time observing nature. He realised he had forgotten nearly every bit of Greek he had learned at school and so he worked hard with a private tutor to be of a good enough standard to enter Christ's College Cambridge in early 1828. Erasmus was also studying there at the time for his Bachelor of Medicine examination, and so was George Fox Darwin, another cousin.

Cambridge had nearly 2,000 resident students at that time, the majority of them rich members of the upper classes without much desire for academic knowledge. It was easy to fall in with the wrong crowd. Charles threw himself

KEYWORD

Botany, the study of plant biology.

into student life, but avoided excess. He realised that he could not compete financially with many of the hunting set he belonged to and avoided many of their escapades. Cousin George was interested in the new craze of 'beetling' and Charles was soon spending most of his spare time collecting beetles in the wild and identifying them. It was through his cousin that Charles met the Reverend John Stevens Henslow, a professor of **botany** who kept open house for any students interested in natural history. They soon became close friends.

Charles became obsessed with beetles and spent the summer break collecting them instead of working on mathematics, which he struggled with. He could not bear to lose out on any specimen and recounts in his autobiography how he found a new beetle while already holding two in his hands. Anxious not to lose the specimen he popped it into his mouth for safekeeping, but it emitted an acrid liquid that was so disgusting he had to spit it out. In the confusion he lost all three specimens.

In the autumn he again enjoyed hunting, and his romance with Fanny flourished. He felt unhappy about returning to Cambridge, especially as Erasmus and George had passed their exams and left to find work. He became aimless again and started to drink more heavily, frittering away his allowance in an attempt to keep up with the richer students. He belonged to the Glutton Club, whose members met to eat 'birds and beasts unknown to the human palate'. One dish they sampled was owl, which was never repeated! Naturally his academic work suffered as a result of his social life.

Student food.

In the summer of 1829 he returned home and was very ill for two weeks. After his illness he decided he would stop wasting his life and make an effort to get on with his studies. In the next academic year he dropped most of his drinking cronies and started to see more of Henslow and his set. He spent so much time with them that he became known as 'that man who walks with Henslow'. It was through this friendship that he became more interested in plants as well as beetles.

His changed ways, however, did not impress his father and they had a blazing row, in the summer holiday of 1830, over his lack of application to his studies. Matters did not improve much when he heard that Fanny, his old sweetheart was engaged to be married to another. He put his energies into his studies at last and eventually passed his BA degree in January 1831, without honours.

As he had to stay at the university until June he spent a great deal of time with Henslow. Henslow loved to travel and recommended that Charles should read Alexander von Humboldt's book, *A Personal Narrative of Travels to the Equinoctial regions of America During the years 1700–1804*. Humboldt was a well known German explorer and his book gave vivid descriptions of his travels in the Canary Isles and around the American continent, describing the many new species of animals he had seen. Travel books were extremely popular in the days before television and films enabled people to see the wonders of the world. Darwin found the book engrossing and longed to travel to the places Humboldt described.

Henslow introduced Charles to the Reverend Adam Sedgwick, a famous geologist, who was researching rock formations around Britain. Charles and Sedgwick visited Wales that summer to study **geology**, and it was here he learnt to recognise rock samples and identify and interpret the rock **strata**. His knowledge of geology was later very useful while on board *The Beagle* and was one of the factors that led to the formulation of his theory of evolution.

KEYWORDS

Geology, the scientific study of the earth's crust.

Strata, layers in rock formation.

Naturalist, student of animals and plants.

When Charles eventually returned home in August 1831 he found a letter from Henslow awaiting him, a letter that would change the course of his whole life. Henslow had been offered a job as a **naturalist** aboard the HMS *Beagle* but his wife did not want him to go as she had just given birth to their first child. Henslow had recommended Charles as a suitable substitute. 'I have stated that I consider you to be the best qualified person I know … amply qualified for collecting, observing and noting anything worthy in Natural History,' he wrote in the letter. Here was a chance to travel around the world if he wanted it; one of his childhood dreams seemed to be coming true.

✳ ✳ ✳ ✳ SUMMARY ✳ ✳ ✳ ✳

- Charles Darwin is a well-known scientist who was born in 1809 and died in 1882.

- He is chiefly remembered for the theory of natural selection, a way of explaining how living things evolve.

- He came from a prosperous and religious family background.

- He was not an outstanding pupil at school but went on to study medicine and theology.

- He was more interested in his hobbies of hunting, geology and natural history than in his academic work.

- His life suddenly changed when he was offered a position abroad the HMS *Beagle* as a naturalist.

The Voyage of *The Beagle* 2

It seems that fate played a great part in shaping the life of the young Darwin, for he was certainly in the right place at the right time. His friendship with Henslow and his obvious love of natural history led to his being considered as a candidate for the post of naturalist on *The Beagle*, despite the fact that he had no formal qualifications in the subject.

The Beagle was a brig, a type of small two-masted warship and had recently been refitted at Plymouth. The British Admiralty was sending her on a voyage around the world for several reasons:

* to survey the South American coast, including Tierra del Fuego;

* to establish the exact **longitude** of Rio de Janeiro;

* to observe and report on the Falkland Islands, a disputed territory between Britain and Argentina;

* to continue around the world via the Galapagos Islands, Tahiti, Australia, St Helena and the Ascension Islands, while making accurate measurements using **chronometers**.

KEYWORDS

Longitude, angular measurement of how far east or west a place is from the Greenwich meridian in London.

Chronometers, very accurate ships' clocks used to compare local and Greenwich time, thus establishing longitude.

World trade was expanding rapidly at the time and it was important that British shipping had good access to foreign ports to enable overseas markets to be exploited. It was also important that the British Navy was seen to be strong in order to protect merchant shipping routes. Survey ships were very important for they had to report back on climate, geology, minerals, inhabitants and the natural flora and fauna of the areas that were visited, as well as creating accurate charts.

The Beagle was also carrying passengers, three natives of Tierra del Fuego, returning there with a missionary, Richard Matthews. They had been captured by the ship's crew on a previous voyage and the captain had them educated in England at his own expense as a kind of religious experiment. He wanted to see if they could convert the natives to Christianity on their return home.

PREPARATION FOR THE VOYAGE

Darwin was keen to go on the voyage but needed his father's approval, for there was no payment for the position of naturalist, indeed, he was even expected to pay for his own passage. His father was understandably dubious about the whole affair, believing it to be a wild scheme and a useless undertaking. He thought something must be wrong with the position for the simple reason that it being offered to someone unqualified at the last minute. He was also worried that Charles would never be able to settle down to a normal life afterwards. Darwin wrote in his autobiography that his father said: 'If you can find any man of common-sense who advises you to go I will give my consent.'

Charles wrote to Henslow saying he would not be able to take up the position, for he knew he would never find any one to consent to such a hare-brained scheme. He set off to Maer to visit his Wedgwood relatives for some shooting instead. Here he was surprised, for the family thought the voyage was a chance not to be missed and Uncle Josiah agreed to return home with him immediately to persuade his father to relent. Robert Darwin had always approved of Josiah's common sense, so he eventually agreed and Charles hurriedly sent off another letter retracting his first refusal.

The person with the final approval for the position was the captain, Robert FitzRoy. It was vital that whoever went along as naturalist was approved of by the captain personally, for they would be living at very close quarters, sharing a cabin and dining together. FitzRoy was only 26 and came from an aristocratic background and he wanted the naturalist to be a young gentleman and companion.

The journey was expected to take at least two years, if not considerably longer. It was important that the captain of a ship did not become too familiar with the crew members if he were to keep discipline, but it was a very long voyage to undertake without companionship. There was none of the modern diversions of television, radio or computer games to while away the long hours and conditions in the cabins were very cramped.

Darwin met Captain FitzRoy in September 1831 and they immediately hit it off although Fitzroy was a believer in **physiognomy** and did not approve of the shape of Darwin's nose, believing it showed a lack of energy and determination. However, he overcame these

KEYWORD

Physiognomy, method of judging a person's character by the shape and size of facial features.

scruples and Darwin was offered the job. *The Beagle* was due to set sail in October 1831 but was delayed, giving Darwin more time to prepare; he spent some time in London learning more about preserving animal and plant specimens at the zoo and the British Museum. He arranged for Henslow to store any specimens that he sent back so that he could sort them on his return. The delay also gave him more time to worry about the journey and he suffered from headaches and heart palpitations, probably as a result of stress. Life at sea would be new to him and could be dangerous and, furthermore, he was leaving behind his loving family whom he might never see again.

Although *The Beagle* had been refitted and the decks had been raised to give more headroom, conditions were still cramped for the crew of 74 seamen, six boys, a surgeon and his assistant, an artist, an instrument maker and a carpenter. The ship set sail on 7 December 1831, and did not return for five years.

THE VOYAGE BEGINS
The Atlantic in winter is not the ideal place for a novice sailor and Darwin suffered terribly from sea sickness. He lay in his hammock for days, barely able to lift his head and existing on a diet of raisins.

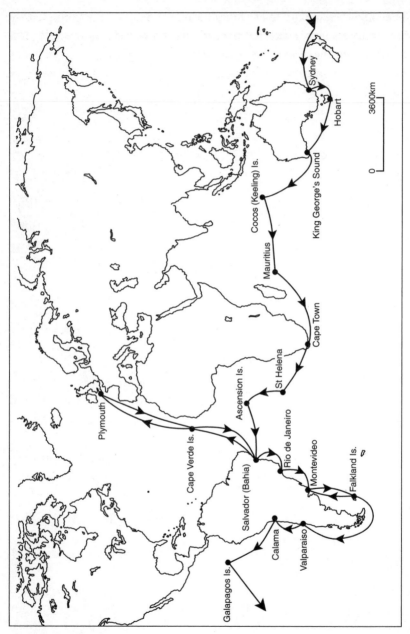

Voyage of The Beagle

Although the captain wrote home, 'I never saw a shore going fellow come into the ways of a ship so soon', Darwin continued to be plagued by sea sickness throughout the journey.

Darwin enjoyed the company of FitzRoy, although he could be rather bad tempered, especially first thing in the morning. The crew called him 'Hot Coffee' because he boiled over easily and they kept out of his way when he looked moody. Despite this Darwin and the captain had only one major disagreement; about slavery, which Darwin didn't approve of.

There was not much for Darwin to do while at sea, so he spent time reading a book that Henslow had given him, Charles Lyell's *Principles of Geology*. Lyell's geological viewpoint differed from most of his contemporaries who believed changes in the earth's surface were due to acts of God. Lyell believed some changes were due to biblical events like the Great Flood, but that others were due to natural forces, such as erosion by wind and water, over long periods of time. Darwin could not agree with this view at first but as he travelled and saw geological evidence he began to believe Lyell could be right. This was an important step towards his theory of evolution, but he did not realise its importance until the voyage had ended.

The other activity which kept him busy was writing his journal, which was published in 1839 under the title *The Journal of Researches into the geology and natural history of the countries visited during the voyage of HMS Beagle*. It was a popular success and it is still in print today. Although the observations made on the journey were very important to Darwin in developing his theory of evolution it is important to remember that:

* He did not recognise the significance of everything he saw while on the voyage.

* The journal was republished in1845 and was revised to emphasise the parts that were seen to be important to the theory of evolution.

ACROSS THE ATLANTIC TO BRAZIL

The ship began its long voyage, encountering fierce storms in the Bay of Biscay that made Darwin long for dry land. However, there were problems in finding a suitable place to dock – they were unable to land at Madeira as the tide was against them and they were unable to land at Tenerife as the islanders thought they could be carrying cholera from England. They finally reached their first land on 16 January 1832, Sao Tiago, part of the Cape Verde islands off the coast of North Africa.

This was Darwin's first glimpse of tropical foliage, although it was nothing compared to what he was to see later. He marvelled at his first sight of a coconut tree and the diversity of the life around him. It was the first time he had seen a volcanic island and he began to take more interest in geology. While on a trip to the interior he found a cliff which had a band of white rock running through it. When he examined it closely he realised the band was made of tiny sea shells. He puzzled over these. How did they get to be so far from the ocean? Perhaps Lyell's theories might be correct and natural phenomena had slowly shaped the earth. He did not come to any conclusions at the time, but wrote in his journal and pondered over it at a later date.

After 23 days the ship continued towards South America and crossed the equator. Anyone who had not crossed before was initiated by the captain, who was dressed as Neptune, shaved with a rusty razor and dunked in a sail full of water by the crew. By this time the sea was calmer and Darwin was becoming more used to life on board ship. He was well liked by the crew, despite the fact that they thought some of his specimens were strange and smelly. They gave him the affectionate names of 'Fly Catcher' and 'The Philosopher'. He was especially friendly with the ship's artist, Augustus Earle, which was useful as Darwin couldn't draw. Many drawings of specimens were made by Earle and by the captain who was a talented amateur artist.

THE EAST COAST OF SOUTH AMERICA, TIERRA DEL FUEGO AND THE FALKLAND ISLANDS

The ship reached Bahia in Brazil in February 1832. This was where the official survey began. *The Beagle* spent two years charting the coast, travelling slowly southwards. It became Darwin's habit to explore inland wherever the

KEYWORD

Gauchos: South American cowboys.

ship docked. He often employed local guides and took whatever accommodation was available. Some of his greatest memories were of sleeping under the stars with the **gauchos**, eating armadillo, drinking *mate* and smoking cigarillos. He made observations and collected specimens, trapping and shooting one day and preserving his finds the following day. He wrote his journal up at night.

His first exploration into the interior was to a coffee plantation north of Rio de Janeiro. It was the first time he had been in a tropical rainforest and his senses were overwhelmed by his surroundings. The air was filled with the aromatic scents of clove and cinnamon, colourful humming birds, toucans and parrots flew above him. 'I never experienced such intense delight', he wrote in a letter to Henslow. It was the insect life that really fascinated him, he collected numerous specimens and noted how many used camouflage to avoid being preyed on. Near Rio he collected 68 different species in one day and wrote to his family: 'I am becoming quite devoted to natural history.'

He collected so many specimens that he needed help and employed a boy, Sims Covington, to help with shooting and stuffing. 'An odd sort of person,' he wrote home, 'perhaps from his very oddity very well adapted to my purposes.' The captain reprimanded him for bringing cargoes of apparent rubbish on board as the specimens piled up in the hold. Darwin carefully packed and labelled everything straightaway, not trusting his memory. He did not really know what most of his finds were and was not even sure if they were reaching Henslow in good condition.

Some of his most thought-provoking finds were fossils uncovered in the bleak wintry landscape of Patagonia. Here he explored Punta Alta, a vast shingle bank with a layer of clay running through it. It was in gravel at the base that he found ancient fossilised bones. At

KEYWORD

Palaeontology, study of life in the distant geological past, usually from fossil remains.

that time very little of the **palaeontology** of South America had been researched, and he was not quite sure what extinct creatures he had found at first. Among his finds were:

* toxodon, a strange rodent, something like a giant capybara;

* macrauchenia, a giant armadillo;

* megatherium, a giant sloth.

These were important finds for they were very similar to creatures that were still alive in the world, the living animals being much smaller. He wondered what had happened to make the giants die out, and why they were lying in a matrix of sea shells. Could it be that the land was rising out of the sea? His notebooks are full of supposition but no conclusions.

In Tierra del Fuego, the southernmost tip of the continent, he wondered about the origins and adaptability of human beings. The ship had stopped here to let the native Fuegians and their missionary on shore. The climate was extremely bleak, for they were close to the Antarctic and the terrain was harsh. Darwin thought the people here were closer to wild animals than to humans. They coated themselves in grease and wore only a mantle of guanaco skin. As the ship approached they watched a woman suckling her baby in a canoe, snow fell and thawed on her naked breast, but she seemed unaware of the cold. He marvelled at their adaptability to their conditions.

He observed how different the 'civilised' Fuegian passengers were in their manners and dress. He could not believe they had once been 'savages'. When the ship later returned to Tierra del Fuego these 'civilised' natives had reverted to their old ways. The religious experiment had failed.

Darwin had plenty of time for observation while visiting the Falkland Islands. The islands were disputed territory and so had to be surveyed accurately, leaving him free to wander about. He spent some time dissecting small plant-like marine animals – corals and zoophytes – and realised there was no real dividing line between animals and plants. He was also fascinated by the geology of the area and took many rock samples.

While in the Falklands he had exciting news from home: Henslow had received the specimens and displayed the fossils before the British Association for the Advancement of Science. Darwin was becoming famous, the fossils were greatly prized and he was overjoyed.

THE WEST COAST OF SOUTH AMERICA AND THE GALAPAGOS

The Beagle set off up the western coast of South America in June 1834. In July they reached Valparaiso and the crew enjoyed the warm Pacific climate. Darwin went exploring in the foothills of the Andes where he discovered more layers of seashells in rocks, hundreds of miles from the sea and parts of a petrified forest lying among marine rock deposits. This reinforced his belief that South America had once been under water and was gradually rising.

He was able to see some of the geological forces that shaped the world when the crew witnessed the eruption of the volcano Osorno in January 1835. It was reported that other volcanoes, over 2,000 miles along the coast, had erupted at about the same time.

Only four weeks later he experienced an earthquake at first hand while on land at Valdivia in Chile. 'The world, the very emblem of all that is solid, had moved beneath our feet, like a crust over fluid,' he wrote in his journal. When he visited the town of Concepcion with FitzRoy, they found it was almost destroyed and the level of the land had been raised considerably. Surely, Darwin reasoned, this might have happened many times before and shaped the surface of the earth.

In September 1835 *The Beagle* reached the Galapagos, a group of volcanic islands off the northwest coast of South America. Here Darwin made some of his most important discoveries, although, again, he did not realise this at the time. The islands have little vegetation, being made of black volcanic rock, and they were used as a penal colony. They were also a well known stopping off point for American whaling ships, useful for their freshwater supplies and inhabited by giant tortoises which the sailors roasted in their shells to feast on the fresh meat.

Darwin and some of the crew were put ashore at James Island and he noticed how the birds and animals were very different from those on the mainland, but still bearing some similarities. When he sorted through his finds later he realised that many were unique, completely new species, but very like mainland ones in some respects.

He eventually realised that the species differed from island to island in a very marked manner although the islands were only 40 miles apart. Darwin noticed this at first with mocking birds and was told by the vice governor that the tortoises were also very different on each island, boasting that he could tell where a tortoise came from just by looking at its shell. Darwin did not look into this as he believed the tortoises were not a natural species to the islands but a recent import, brought to the islands by sailors as food. Any tortoises that were taken onto *The Beagle* were eaten and the shells were thrown overboard, so he had no chance of researching the differences until much later.

The most frequently quoted differences among species that he noted was the shape of the beaks of the islands' finches. On one island the beaks of the finches were thick, for cracking nuts and seeds. On another island they were small, to enable the birds to catch insects; on yet another island they were adapted to feed on fruits and flowers. This became one of the best known examples of the way in which animals adapt to their habitats, but again he didn't notice it at the time and many of his specimens were not labelled as being from separate islands.

Later, when he returned home, he needed help to sort them out and it was then that the important discovery was made.

'You want the shells?'

AUSTRALIA AND HOME

The Beagle reached Australia in January 1836, by way of Tahiti and New Zealand. On one of his inland trips he saw his first marsupial, a pota-roo, and he examined the body of a platypus. He puzzled over this odd cross between a mammal and a reptile. There was still a scientific debate raging about whether or not they laid eggs.

In April 1836 they reached the Keeling or Cocos islands in the Indian Ocean where he saw his first coral atoll, a circular reef surrounding a lagoon. He had a theory that if South America was rising then the land under the South Seas might possibly be sinking. He reasoned that the atolls were formed as the islands sank and the corals grew upwards towards the light. At the bottom they would be dead and at the top they would form a living fringe around the circular lagoon. FitzRoy took soundings from the ship to try and determine the depth at which the coral began to grow but they reached 7,000 feet without finding the bottom and could not measure any further. Darwin believed that this supported his theory and he wrote a paper on it after his return home.

The Beagle returned to England via Mauritius, the Cape of Good Hope, and St Helena. Everyone was desperate to return, for the journey had taken nearly five years but FitzRoy, a great perfectionist, had decided to return to Bahia to take check the longitude readings.

Eventually they reached Falmouth in England on the 2 October, 1836. The sailor's life had ended for Darwin but he had plenty to show for it. He had a diary of 770 pages, a geology notebook of 1,383 pages and a zoology notebook of 368 pages. His specimen catalogue listed 1,529 preserved in spirits and 3,907 skins, bones and dried objects. His work was only just beginning.

✳ ✳ ✳ ✳ SUMMARY ✳ ✳ ✳ ✳

- Darwin was accepted by Captain FitzRoy of *The Beagle* and became the ship's naturalist in 1831.

- *The Beagle* was a survey ship and was making a round-the-world voyage.

- While on board Darwin read Lyell's *Principles of Geology* and this influenced his thinking about the way the earth was formed and had developed.

- While the ship's crew carried out coastal surveys, Darwin visited the interior of many countries collecting specimens.

- In South America he discovered the fossils of large extinct mammals that bore strong resemblances to animals still living, except for their size.

- He found examples of fossilized sea life high in the mountains and wondered if the land had risen.

- He collected many interesting bird specimens in the Galapagos Islands. These were highly adapted to the conditions in which they lived, but he didn't realise it at the time.

- By the time he returned home in 1836 he had amassed a great number of plant and animal specimens to be investigated.

Towards a Theory of Evolution 3

When Darwin returned to England in 1836 he spent a short time at home in Shropshire with his family, but he knew that to make any impression on the scientific world he would have to move to London. His father resigned himself to the fact that his son would never become a clergyman and gave him a generous allowance so that he wouldn't have to earn a living. Darwin divided his time between Cambridge, where he sorted out the specimens he had sent home to Henslow, and London where he tried to get expert advice on his finds.

The Zoological Society was rather over-whelmed with specimens that had been sent in by naturalists from other survey ships and from the new colonies. It was difficult to find anyone who had the time to examine his finds properly. His bird collection ended up in the

hands of John Gould, a bird expert, who realised that the badly labelled birds from the Galapagos were all finches. Darwin hadn't realised this as they all looked so different and had different shaped beaks. He had thought they were completely different species. This gave him food for thought. What caused these differences and how had the birds arrived at the islands in the first place? He did not suddenly 'discover' an explanation for evolution but spent years puzzling over the things he had seen. He knew that the world must have changed over time and believed that the living things on it must have changed too, otherwise they would have died out as conditions changed. In 1837 he began notebooks on the **transmutation** of species, but only mentioned his theories to a few close friends.

Publicly he was becoming well known as a geologist. He met with Lyell and became a member of the Geological Society in London, where he read a paper on his theory that the land in South America was slowly rising. This was well received and he eventually went on to publish more geological papers, including one on the formation of coral reefs and several on the geology of volcanic regions he had visited. He was eventually made secretary of the Geological Society and was elected to the Council of the Royal Geographic Society.

He was also becoming a well-known author: his family had enjoyed reading his journal from *The Beagle* and they persuaded him to publish it in book form. He did this in 1839 and it became a popular success with armchair travellers and made him famous. He also obtained funding for the *Zoology of Beagle* which was published with the assistance of other well known naturalists. This came out in five volumes over several years. All the time that this work was going on he still continued to make secret notes on evolution.

The theory of evolution did not come to Darwin in a blinding flash. His notebooks show a gradual groping towards his final position on the subject. His eventual publication *On the Origin of Species* did not come out until 1859. Because he saw that previous writers on evolution had been ridiculed by the scientific community he was very cautious. He also worried about the implication of his ideas on the hierarchical Christian society that he lived in.

EVOLUTION BEFORE DARWIN

Long before Darwin was born people were trying to make sense of the world around them and to understand how it had come about. Where did man and animals come from? How did life begin? Who created the world? The first explanations were religious or supernatural ones. Around the world there are as many different stories of how life began as there are religions.

Creationist Theory

In western Europe old pagan beliefs were superseded by the Christian faith and its chief teachings, *The Bible*. *The Bible* states that God made the world. 'Out of the ground the Lord God formed every beast of the field, and every fowl of the air.' *The Bible* also claims that the first man,

Adam, was created in God's image and the first woman, Eve, was created from one of Adam's ribs. After the creation the world remained unchanged, until God punished man by sending a great flood. Noah and his family escaped by building an ark and the animal kingdom was saved because Noah took a breeding pair of every kind of animal on board. The orthodox Christian belief was that the world hadn't changed since then, everything in the world was as God intended it to be when he created it. This became known as **creationist** theory.

KEYWORDS

Creationist, theory that the world was created not by random events but by divine intervention.

Fossils, ancient remains of plants and animals hardened into rock.

Invertebrates, creatures without backbones.

This version of events was accepted by most people until the 18th century when philosophers and scientists began to question what *The Bible* said and were able to voice these ideas without immediately being burned at the stake! What made them think was scientific evidence that did not fit in with the ideas of the creationists.

The Fossil Record

Fossils had puzzled people for a long time, what were they? Could they possibly be the bones of long dead creatures? If this were so then *The Bible* might not be literally true, for as the naturalist John Ray (1627–1705) pointed out, fossil bones had been found belonging to creatures that were no longer alive; so everything in the world was not as God created it. As more fossil layers were discovered they showed that the earliest life had been that of **invertebrates**, for these were found in the oldest layers; then fish appeared followed by reptiles, birds, mammals and, finally, man.

Creationists believed that the fossils showed that God had punished the world with several catastrophes and had each time made the world anew. There had been several acts of creation and not just one. The biblical story of Noah in his ark was just the last in a line of punishments that God had sent to the world, each time remaking it.

Progressionism developed from these ideas, the theory proposing that the reason that different types of creatures existed in different fossil layers was that God had created the world in a series of stages. First he created invertebrates, then fish, etc. Progressionists did not believe that the species had evolved from each other. They saw each stage as a distinctly separate part of life on earth. This was reinforced by the geological belief of

catastrophism developed by Georges Cuvier (1769–1832). He believed that the history of the earth's crust was one of violent cataclysms such as earthquakes, volcanoes and floods that had shaped its surface. He believed that fossils were the remains of these catastrophes. In this he was partly right, but the forces that have created the world we live in are much more complex than this.

EVOLUTIONARY THINKERS

Although the majority of people followed religious doctrine and sub-scribed to the creationist view, there were others who believed that life must have evolved from earlier forms; at first they had no evidence to support their beliefs so they were not taken seriously by the scientific community.

Georges-Louis Leclerc, (comte de) Buffon (1707–1788)

Buffon, who became a naturalist, was born in Burgundy, France. He was the first scientist to publish ideas that questioned creationism. Buffon believed that God had created most of the animals in the world, but in addition there were types that had been produced by processes of nature over a period of time. He thought that donkeys were a kind of degenerative offspring from horses and that monkeys were a result of a similar degeneration from mankind. He also thought that the world was much older than was commonly believed at the time. Scholars had been working this out from *The Bible*; in the 17th century Archbishop James Ussher claimed the date of the creation was 4004BC.

This belief persisted for many years and was used as an important argument against evolution, for if changes to species had occurred it must have taken hundreds of thousands of years. Buffon also realised that animals competed with each other in a struggle for survival because of the rate at which they reproduced but, unlike Darwin, didn't really draw any conclusions from the idea.

Erasmus Darwin (1731–1802)

Erasmus Darwin was Charles' paternal grandfather and was a famous physician and poet. Like Buffon he also realised that animals lived in competition with each other in a struggle for survival and that the environment was an important factor in the way species might change. As a botanist he was chiefly interested in the evolution of plants. He is famous for *Zoonomia, or, the Laws of Organic Life*, a written work that expresses these views. His ideas on evolution were very different from those of his grandson but they must have influenced his outlook to some extent.

Jean Baptiste Lamarck (1744–1829)

Lamarck was a French naturalist who invented the term biology and was a great scholar of the subject, but he is most famous for his work on evolution. He questioned the idea of the great chain of being, an eighteenth century philosophical view of the way life was ordered. This view saw nature as something like a ladder where every living thing had a fixed place. At the bottom were simple plants, on the rung above simple animals, then reptiles, birds, mammals and man. Man stood about halfway up the ladder and above him were different types of angels. At the top of the ladder was God. This view of an orderly nature was popular because it showed that everything had a fixed place in the structure of things according to the will of God. It could be seen as a model for the way that society should work, everyone in their ordained place, with the rich at the top and the poor at the bottom. Lamarck adapted this view: in his view the ladder was not static but a constantly moving upward progression. Instead of God, man was the ideal at the top of the ladder, and all the creatures below were trying to develop

into humans. Lamarck thought that life could be spontaneously gener-
ated from inanimate matter as it progressed upwards on the ladder due
to an inbuilt force that made it want to better itself until it reached the
complexity of man. Man was the pinnacle of evolution as God intended when he set the forces of nature into motion. As evidence of this
Lamarck pointed out that fossils in older layers of rock were less developed than those in more recent layers.

Lamarck's explanation of how the creatures evolved up the ladder was
mistaken, but part of his theory of evolution was based on a sound
observation, for he believed the environment was an important factor
in the way animals evolved.

He is well known for his erroneous suggestion
that animals could generate new organs or
structures to meet their needs and pass these
on to their offspring. As an example Lamarck
used the giraffe. He believed that the animal's

KEYWORD

Genetics, study of heredity
and variation.

long neck was a result of it stretching up to reach leaves at the top of
trees, this characteristic then being passed on to future generations.
This theory was plausible at the time for nobody understood **genetics**
and scientists did not know how characteristics were inherited.
Lamarck also believed that the opposite effect would also happen, if an
organ or structure were not used it would shrink and this characteristic would also be passed on.

The suggestion that one species had developed out of another and that
man had arisen out of another species caused controversy and outrage.
Lamarck was derided by the church and ridiculed by the scientists of
the time, who believed catastrophism was the reason for the fossil
record. He died a pauper and was buried in an unmarked grave.
Although much of his theory was mistaken Lamarck is important
because he put the idea of evolution forward in a forceful way and tried
to justify his theory.

Evolution of the giraffe.

Robert Chambers (1802–1871)

Robert Chambers is not well known as an evolutionist because his most famous work was published anonymously. He was an author, mainly of reference books and encyclopaedias; his brother, William Chambers, was the Edinburgh publisher. *The Vestiges of the Natural History of Creation* was published in 1844 amid public outcry. Of course it sold well because of this, running into 11 editions. The fact that it was anonymous led to much speculation about the author. Was it Charles Lyell the geologist or Lord Byron's daughter? There was even a rumour that the author was Prince Albert, the husband of Queen Victoria! The true identity of the author was not revealed until after his death, although some people had guessed before that.

Vestiges was only a short pamphlet but it made the discussion of evolution very popular. Chambers pointed out that the succession of fossil types indicated that species must have evolved rather than having been suddenly created. The scientific world ridiculed the idea and the scandal that the book caused may have been one of the reasons that Darwin kept his ideas secret for so long. He was determined to gather as much evidence as possible so that nobody could call his work unscientific.

MARRIAGE AND COUNTRY LIFE

While Darwin was working on his public scientific theories and his private notebooks he began to wonder if he should get married. In July1838 he made a table of the advantages and disadvantages of being married. This seems rather cold blooded, especially the entry 'object to be beloved and played with – better than a dog anyhow', but Darwin actually became a devoted husband and loving father. He married his cousin, Emma Wedgwood, in January 1839 and they had ten children. In his autobiography he wrote: 'She has been my greatest blessing and I can declare that in my whole life I have never heard her utter one word I would rather have been unsaid.' She was a great support to Darwin for she nursed him constantly throughout his illness, supported his views, dealt with accounts and correspondence in addition to her role as a mother.

Emma was a devout Christian but Darwin was quite open about his ideas on evolution at the beginning of their marriage. A letter written by Emma in 1839 shows that she was worried about the way his ideas were progressing but she admired his honesty in telling her his beliefs.

At first the Darwins lived in London so that Charles could be near his work, but problems with his health meant that the family started to look for a place in the country; they moved to Downe, near Bromley, in Kent in 1842. There has been much debate over what kind of illness Darwin suffered from – his main symptoms were palpitations of the heart, headaches, skin problems, aching joints, nausea and insomnia. There are several theories to explain them:

* He had a tropical disease, probably Chagas disease, which he picked up on his voyage around the world.

* His illness was psychosomatic, brought on by the worry of the controversy about his theories or by the influence of an overbearing father.

* He suffered from stress, overwork and eyestrain.

* He was suffering arsenic poisoning as a result of using Fowler's Solution, which his father is known to have prescribed for him.

* He was suffering from some other physical illness or allergic reaction which couldn't be diagnosed at the time.

Nobody can really be certain about any of this, but it is generally felt that the illness had some connection to his mental state for he suffered the symptoms just before *The Beagle* departed and the more extreme attacks seemed to occur when he was under stress. He had been extremely fit when young, climbing the Andes and roaming the pampas with the gauchos; early portraits show a robust young man but the picture most people have of Darwin is of a sickly, bearded old man.

He is also generally believed to have been a recluse but this is not strictly true. Although he moved out of London, he was only 16 miles away and he still visited when his health permitted. Although he withdrew from many of the societies he belonged to because of his illness he still kept up a vast correspondence with his scientific peers.

Although his illness slowed him down physically it did not stop him from working on his transmutation notebooks and carrying out experiments in his own house and garden. He had a strict routine that enabled him to carry out his work with the support of his family and servants. He had a private study where he worked after breakfast from 8.00–9.30, he would then read letters or have a novel read to him until 10.30. He was very fond of novels with romantic heroines, his favourite novelists were Jane Austen and Mrs Gaskell. He would work until lunchtime when, at 12.00, he took a walk in the garden, whatever the weather, before his lunch. He often examined his experimental plants in the greenhouse before he walked around the 'thinking path' as he called it. It was here that he mulled over his ideas. After lunch he read the paper and replied to correspondence. At 3.00 he would have a rest and read another instalment from a novel, then he would walk outside for half an hour before working in his study for an hour. He would then spend half an hour in the drawing room with his family, have another rest until dinner at 7.30 and after dinner play backgammon with Emma and listen to her play the piano. He always went to bed at 10.30 although he often slept badly. This routine was nearly always kept to unless he felt really ill and was to continue until the end of his life.

Darwin was a slow and methodical worker, this could have been a result of the restrictions placed upon him by illness but his notebooks on transmutation show how important he felt it was to have a theory that would stand up to the scrutiny of the finest scientific minds. He became increasingly certain that his ideas were correct but he had to prove them, even if it meant devoting his whole life to the cause.

✳ ✳ ✳ ✳ SUMMARY ✳ ✳ ✳ ✳

- Darwin began notebooks on the transmutation of species in 1837 and in these he finally formulated the theory of evolution.

- He only told a few very close family and friends of his ideas.

- While working on his secret notebooks he became well known as an author, a naturalist and a geologist.

- He became ill and was an invalid for most of his life. No one knows what caused his illness but there may have been some psychological factors.

- Darwin's ideas went against those of the established Christian church which believed God had created the world and all the animals and plants to a divine plan.

- Other evolutionary thinkers before him were Buffon, Lamarck and Erasmus Darwin.

- Robert Chambers published a pamphlet on evolution while Darwin was working on his theory. It was ridiculed by the scientific community and caused a social scandal.

- Darwin worked slowly on his theories and gathered as much proof as he could in order that they would not be dismissed.

Darwin's Theory of Evolution 4

Despite his bouts of ill health Darwin continued to work on his transmutation notebooks.
In 1842 he wrote a 35-page essay on the subject
and locked it away in a drawer. He developed
his ideas into a 230-page essay by 1844 and left

instructions for it to be published in the event of his death. In this
document the main theories that were to become the *Origin of Species*
in 1859 were formulated, although he continued to update his work in
the light of the experiments and observations that he continued to
make. The main argument of Darwin's transmutation theory was that
all animals had evolved from a common ancestor over a long period of
time; because the world had changed a great deal during this time
living things had to change in order to survive. In his notebook Darwin
sketched a branching tree to illustrate the way he believed life had
developed from a common ancestor, every branch was a new species
that continued to divide as more and more species were produced.
Eventually the tree branches would be so dense that it would be
difficult to see how they had developed from the main stem. His
thoughts on this may well have been influenced by the findings of
Franz Bopp, a **philologist**. In 1816 he had proposed that all European
languages were descended from the same Indo-European root
language.

We saw in Chapter 3 how others before Darwin had tried unsuccess-
fully to convert people to the idea of evolution. Darwin's theory
differed from these in two main ways:

* the mechanism of natural selection which attempted to explain *how*
  evolution occurred, and;

* the amount of evidence and observation he used to support his
  theory.

NATURAL SELECTION

Darwin saw evidence that plants and animals had changed a great deal since the beginning of the world. He believed that the earth's **species** had evolved from other forms into their present forms and that they would continue to evolve. The process by which they evolved he called natural selection.

He saw that each species produces more offspring than can survive in a given environment due to the pressures on the amount of food available. There is great competition between members of a species to survive, any advantage that an individual can gain helps it to beat others in this struggle and makes it more fit to survive.

Nature provides some individuals with these advantages. The stronger, more fit members in a species are more likely to survive and reproduce; they will pass on their survival characteristics to their offspring, Members of a species without these advantages are more likely to die out.

In the *Origin of Species* the term **survival of the fittest** is used, leading people to believe that Darwin was suggesting that it was natural for the strong to overcome the weak. For Darwin the 'fittest' animals were not necessarily the strongest, merely the ones which were most fit to survive and reproduce, for Darwin believed it was sexual reproduction that led to variations in a species.

Plants that are reproduced by cuttings cannot be distinguished from the parent plant but the offspring of two parents are different from their parents and from one another. Sometimes the differences in the offspring have been inherited from the parents but very occasionally completely random variations can occur. These random variations can be passed on through successive generations and any changes which are greatly beneficial may eventually become permanent. Because life is a

KEYWORDS

Species, a group of similar plants or animals that are able to produce fertile offspring.

Survival of the fittest, a phrase invented by Herbert Spencer (1820–1903). In the struggle for survival the fittest will live to reproduce.

struggle for survival those born with favourable characteristics will survive and those without them will die out.

An example which is often used to demonstrate the way this theory works in practice is that of the peppered moth in Britain. The peppered moth uses camouflage to escape from predators. Before the Industrial Revolution occurred the majority of these moths were a light colour and blended in with the lichen that grew on tree trunks. Any darker variants were easily spotted by birds and tended to be eaten.

When factories began spewing out smoke and soot the position reversed itself. Now the tree trunks were darker because soot killed the lichen which grew on the trees. The dark moths were now the ones with the favourable characteristics and were more likely to live to pass them on, so the numbers of dark moths increased over the generations. However, since the 1950s the decline of heavy industry and anti-pollution legislation has meant that the air is much cleaner again. Lichen is growing back so light coloured moths are gradually replacing the dark ones and becoming the more common type.

Darwin began to formulate the theory of natural selection in 1838, when reading *An Essay on the Principle of Population* by Thomas Malthus (1766–1834). Malthus was an English clergyman and political economist. His essay made the point that populations grew by geometrical progression and would increase faster than the means of subsistence, in other words if people didn't stop breeding they would starve to death.

Darwin recognized that despite the theories of Malthus adult populations tended to remain fairly stable from generation to generation. Many species have a high reproductive potential but not all the individuals in a species survive to reproduce. He realised that the struggle for survival did not take place just between different species but between all the individuals in the species, so he became interested in the factors that led to some individuals in a population being successful in surviving.

Darwin knew farmers could select which animals to breed from in order to pass on desired characteristics and realised that nature could select individuals for breeding, but in a different way to humans. The fittest and most able to survive would live to reproduce more successfully. Natural selection would not be as precise as artificial selection. Stock breeders can actively weed out any undesirable traits by culling and by breeding only from true types. In nature individuals with only slightly less desirable characteristics would survive and would produce some offspring. The undesirable traits that the offspring inherit would take some time to disappear from the population. Those individuals that had traits that were definitely to their disadvantage would leave no offspring so those traits would obviously die out more quickly.

Darwin realised there must be natural variations in the population that appeared at random. New variations could spread through the population, over long periods of time if they gave some selective advantage. We saw in Chapter 3 that Lamarck believed the giraffe had acquired a long neck by stretching. Darwin's explanation of the long neck is different from Lamarck's. If a giraffe with a long neck finds it easier to obtain food then those giraffes that are fortunate enough to be born with longer necks will be able to get more food and will be stronger. They are more likely to reproduce successfully and some of their offspring would probably be born with long necks. (Darwin did not understand how the mechanism of inheritance worked, but knew that domestic animals could be bred to develop certain useful characteristics and from that he inferred that there was some way that the long neck could be passed on.)

The offspring born with longer necks would be more successful than those with shorter necks and would again get more food, be stronger and breed more successfully. Over many generations long necks would be favoured so that each succeeding generation would be composed of more animals with long necks than in preceding generations. At some stage there would be a point where it was not physically possible for the neck to grow any longer, due to the ability of the heart to pump blood to the brain, for example.

EVIDENCE AND OBSERVATION AT HOME

Down House had a large garden and it was here that Darwin carried out many experiments on plants and animals:

* to establish his reputation as a serious scientist;
* to develop his transmutation theory.

Barnacles

Darwin became interested in barnacles during the voyage of *The Beagle* when he discovered an unusual type off the Chilean coast. He spent many years studying and classifying all the common types of barnacles and published a two-volume work on the subject. He had a great number of species of barnacles and was able to observe that although the adult forms all appeared to be very different the larvae all looked similar. He wondered if this was because they had a common ancestor. Barnacles were such a common thing around the house that one of his sons became very puzzled when visiting a friend. Where were the barnacles? He thought that every father had a room for dissecting barnacles!

The barnacles were important chiefly because they established Darwin as a serious scientist and not merely a dabbler. The publication of his papers on the subject meant that the scientific world could see he was capable of proper biological investigation.

Domestication and selective breeding

It was well known that farmers and animal breeders could carefully select animals and breed them together in order to pass on any desirable features or temperament. The offspring of cows that gave high milk yields have been bred for thousands of years so that we have excellent breeds of dairy cattle today. Dogs with widely differing features have been bred for different kinds of work, or for show. The same is also true of plants – domesticated cabbages, for instance, were bred from wild straggly plants over the centuries.

Darwin became interested in this **artificial selection**, and thought it would have some bearing on his transmutation theory. He spent a lot of time studying manuals on poultry and pig breeding, visiting agricultural shows and corresponding with breeders. He eventually carried out his own breeding programme using ornamental pigeons and discussed his findings with other pigeon fanciers. He also examined the skeletons of many animals: dogs, rabbits, pigs and fish among others.

> **KEYWORD**
>
> Artificial selection, selection of animals or plants by breeders in order to develop desired characteristics in the offspring.

Sexual selection

Darwin saw that individuals within the same species also had a struggle for survival against members of the same sex. Adult males compete against each other for female partners which often leads to fighting. He also noted that female birds often choose males which display bright or elaborate plumage. He thought that many species had evolved different forms for males and females due to the pressures of sexual selection: 'That is by an individual having had in successive generations some slight advantage over other males, in their weapons, means of defence or charms, which they have transmitted to their male offspring.' His programme of pigeon breeding and experiments included observation of mating displays, but he also tried dyeing pigeons different colours to see if they were attractive to possible mates.

Seed dispersal

Darwin had noted that the plants on the Galapagos were similar to those on the mainland of South America and he became interested in the way that seeds were distributed around the world. He did many experiments, including:

* **Water dispersal**. He tried putting seeds in salt water and freezing them in snow to see if they would still germinate. He also tried to calculate the speed of sea currents in the Atlantic.

* **Bird dispersal**. He examined mud on birds' feet to see if it contained seeds, and analysed their droppings to see if digestion stopped seeds from germinating.

Plant experiments

Darwin spent some time crossing varieties of peas and experimenting with pruning techniques, growing under different colours of glass and under widely differing conditions.

Many scientists at the time believed that plants reproduced without any kind of sexual fertilisation at all. Darwin believed some kind of sexual reproduction must take place in order for variations to occur. He spent a great deal of time studying orchids which have strange shaped petals to guide insects to the correct place in the plant for fertilisation to take place. He eventually produced a work on the subject in 1862. He also became interested in flesh eating plants such as Venus flytraps and sundews and carried out many experiments, feeding them on different substances.

Other evidence and observations

Darwin's lively mind made use of all the experimental evidence he collected at home but he also made connections with everything he had observed on his journey, books he had read and current scientific theory. This was what made his theory so compelling, for he drew in many threads to make a completed work. Many of the ideas were not new but he connected them together in a way that shed a new light on evolution. There were four main areas that he found to support his ideas:

* evidence from *The Beagle*;

* fossil evidence;

* geological theories;

* biological observations made by others.

EVIDENCE FROM THE BEAGLE

Darwin was able to use observations from his travels to support his theory. The specimens that he gathered on the Galapagos were a fundamental part of his theory on the formation of new species. Creationists believed that all species had been created by God. When explorers had discovered the New World in the sixteenth and seventeenth centuries new species were discovered that were not mentioned at all in *The Bible* so creationists had to believe there had been some kind of special creation for the newly discovered continents of Australia and America.

Darwin believed that migration and evolution explained the distribution of living things. He had visited many groups of islands and found few resemblances between life on different groups of islands. For example, the birds on the Cape Verde islands were very different from those on the Galapagos islands. If they had been made to a divine plan, as creationists believed, they could be expected to be very similar, for their environments were very similar.

However, the birds of Cape Verde were very similar to birds on the nearby African continent and the birds of the Galapagos were similar to those of nearby South America. Darwin believed that this was due to migration from the mainland: because the populations of the islands were relatively isolated they developed into new species that bore some relationship to their common ancestors on the mainland. Darwin saw that new species evolve when existing species are separated into isolated groups. Because the environment favours certain characteristics after many generations these groups will have become so different they will no longer be able to interbreed. They have become new species.

The finches of the Galapagos
The best example of this theory is that of the Galapagos finches. Darwin had collected 13 different types and at first believed them to be completely different kinds of birds because they looked so different. The most striking difference was in their beaks. Each had a different type of beak that was adapted to the way in which they obtained food. Seed eating finches have big powerful beaks to crush the seeds, insect-eating finches have thin pointed beaks to pick at tree bark, one variety had even adapted to drink blood.

The Galapagos islands are isolated from each other by powerful ocean currents and have all developed different habitats. The finches are probably evolved from one species that arrived by chance from South America, borne on the wind or ocean currents. Each of the current species adapted to the habitat on their island and developed a different type of beak. Similar differences were also seen in the tortoises and plant life.

The beaks of finches are adapted to their diet.

South American rheas

When travelling the vast pampas of South America during his time with the gauchos, Darwin had discovered that each geographical area had its own type of rhea, a flightless bird rather like an ostrich. Each type was similar but they bore enough differences to be able to tell them apart and one type gradually replaced another as they roamed the area. As he worked on his notebooks Darwin realised that this was because the primitive ancestors of these birds had migrated away from each other and the geographical separation led to new adaptations taking place in the different groups of birds. Eventually they had evolved into new species.

FOSSIL EVIDENCE

We have seen how the discovery of fossils led others before Darwin to question the idea that God had created the world. At the time Darwin was writing there were many new discoveries of fossils and gaps in the fossil record were being filled in. Darwin had observed fossils at first hand in South America.

* The fossils appeared to be in layers, invertebrates appearing first, humans last. This progression would be consistent with evolution.

* Some ancient fossils had been found that were indistinguishable from living animals, so Darwin could argue that the theory of catastrophism could not be right, all animals had not been wiped out by acts of God and then made anew.

* Fossils were discovered that showed intermediate stages between animals from the past and living creatures. The first fossilised **archaeopteryx** was discovered in 1863, this showed the development of feathers and the wing in a transition between dinosaurs and birds, something Darwin had previously predicted.

> **KEYWORD**
>
> Archaeopteryx, primitive, part reptilian bird.

GEOLOGICAL THEORIES

Darwin had been converted to the geological views of Charles Lyell while on board *The Beagle*. Lyell believed the present appearance of the earth was due to uniform geological change over very long periods of time. Darwin reasoned that if the earth had evolved in this way then the living things on it must have done the same, otherwise the environment would be unsuitable for them. Despite his use of Lyell's theory Lyell himself was not totally convinced by Darwin's belief in evolution although they became good friends.

BIOLOGICAL OBSERVATIONS

Biologists and anatomists had made many discoveries about the design and structure of animals. Darwin used some of these findings in the *Origin of Species* to support his theory that all animals were descended from a common ancestor.

Embryological development

As embryos develop they go through stages which resemble the adult forms of more primitive types of animals. Reptile, bird and mammal embryos look very similar during some stages of their development. Although this had been discovered by the eighteenth century it was interpreted as evidence that all animals had one divine creator. Darwin believed this showed that they had all evolved from a common ancestor at some stage in the past.

The common plan

> What can be more curious than that the hand of a man formed for grasping, that of a mole for digging, the leg of a horse, the paddle of the porpoise, and the wing of the bat should all be constructed on the same pattern, and should include similar bones in the same relative positions.
>
> Darwin wrote in the *Origin of Species*

He believed this suggested descent from a common ancestor although those who believed in divine creation believed it showed the existence of some kind of plan.

Darwin argued that the bones of animals had been modified, lengthened, shortened, thickened, etc., to adapt to the different environments that animals lived in and the purposes for which they were used. For example, a horse has an extremely modified forelimb. In man there are five sets of bones that form the hand and fingers, in the horse these have been modified into one set which are thick enough to take the weight of the horse as it runs.

Rudimentary Organs

In Darwin's time it was well known that many animals possessed **rudimentary** or **atrophied** organs. One example given by Darwin was that of certain snakes which have the remains of rudimentary limbs and a pelvis. He also point-

KEYWORDS

Rudimentary, undeveloped part or organ.

Atrophied, wasted away.

ed out that many rudimentary organs are seen in embryos but they disappear later; for example, plankton-eating whales do not have teeth but their embryos do.

Creationists had no other explanation of these other than they existed for the sake of symmetry or to complete the scheme of nature. Darwin was disparaging about this in the *Origin of Species*: 'This is not an explanation, merely a restatement of the fact.' He saw these organs as proof that living creatures had descended from a common ancestor. As animals adapted to different environments they had gradually lost the primitive organs they had once needed.

✳ ✳ ✳ ✳SUMMARY✳ ✳ ✳ ✳

- Darwin worked on his transmutation notebooks and by 1844 he had formulated a theory of evolution.

- He did not publish the theory until 1859 but he let close friends and family know of his work.

- His theory was different from those that went before because he gave supporting evidence to back up his claims.

- He believed that evolution took place by the mechanism of natural selection; animals and plants compete against each other to live.

- The most fit to survive and reproduce live to produce offspring. This is called survival of the fittest.

- Darwin worked at home to try and explain the theory. He did experiments with barnacles, pigeon breeding, seed dispersal and plant breeding.

- He also made use of other supporting evidence that was available at the time and observations he had made on *The Beagle*.

The *Origin of Species*

By 1856 Darwin had filled numerous notebooks with speculation on the transmutation of species. He had discussed his ideas with some of his friends in the scientific community but was still not ready to go public. In May he began writing a book which he called *Natural Selection*. This was a very long and wordy document – by 1858 he had written ten chapters, but it was nowhere near completion. The work progressed slowly as he was still suffering from bouts of very bad health and spent a lot of time taking water cures at several spas around Britain. Lyell and others urged him to publish his ideas before somebody else came up with the theory but he was determined to have as much evidence as possible before he presented his controversial theory to the scrutiny of the scientific world.

In June 1858 he received a bombshell in the form of a letter from a naturalist, Alfred Russell Wallace. Wallace knew that Darwin was interested in the transmutation of species and sent him a 40 page paper that he had written on the subject. As he read it Darwin became horrified, the ideas were almost the same as his own. He wrote a letter to Lyell, bemoaning this 'striking coincidence' and complaining: 'My originality, whatever it may amount to, will be smashed.'

THE INFLUENCE OF WALLACE

Alfred Wallace came from quite a poor family but he was intelligent and had worked his way up in the world to become a collector and naturalist. While recovering from a bout of malaria in Malaysia he worked out a theory of evolution by natural selection very similar to Darwin's.

Like Darwin he had been impressed by the work of Malthus on population and applied it to the natural world. He saw that forms of a species that were poorly adapted to their environment would die out and that the well-adapted ones would survive.

Darwin had been working on his theory for 20 years and was understandably dismayed by Wallace's letter – to gain recognition in the scientific community you need to be the first to publish your ideas. Darwin felt that his work would all be for nothing as Wallace's ideas were in a form that was much more suitable for publication than his own lengthy tome. He asked Lyell for advice and it was decided that a joint paper, bearing the names of Darwin and Wallace, would be read at the Linnaean Society in London, during July. Lyell also arranged that some of Darwin's earlier letters on the subject were produced as evidence to show his precedent. The paper was titled *On the Tendency of Species to Form Varieties* and, as it was largely ignored by the scientific community and was not presented to the public, it caused no controversy.

Some people believe Wallace was badly treated by Darwin and his friends. Some researchers even claim Darwin received Wallace's paper earlier than he claimed and plagiarised Wallace's ideas. There are two main reasons why this is probably not the case:

* Wallace himself believed Darwin was being fair and they became good friends. Surely he would have accused him at the time if he thought he had been plagiarised?

* When examined closely the two theories, although similar, have differences, especially in their ideas on the formation of varieties.

Would Darwin ever have published his theories if it was not for the spur of this rival publication? It is difficult to say, as he seemed to be waiting for the 'right time' to publish but this might never have occurred. Wallace's paper gave him the impetus to come forward with his theory and also greatly affected the form of the publication. Darwin scrapped his long book and used it the basis for a shorter, more succinct work.

On the *Origin of Species*
The book was published in November 1859. *On the Origin of Species by Means of Natural Selection: or the Preservation of Favoured Races in the*

Struggle for Life was the original, full title. Only 1,250 copies were printed at first, since the publisher did not know if it would sell. It sold out on the first day, went in to six editions and is still in print today. As later editions were produced Darwin amended parts of the work as his experiments progressed. The sixth edition, published in 1872, differs substantially from the first and contains a chapter dealing with objections raised by other scientists.

A BRIEF OUTLINE OF THE BOOK

The final version of the book contains 15 chapters. There is no substitute for reading the book but this very brief outline is included to give some idea of the way the argument for natural selection was presented.

The Introduction explains how Darwin came to write the book and how he believes there is no proper explanation of how adaptations occur.

Chapter 1, Variation under Domestication, gives examples of how animal and plant breeders produce different types of domesticated species by the use of artificial selection. Pigeons are given as an example.

Chapter 2, Variation under Nature, demonstrates the variability of wild species. Darwin makes the point that naturalists cannot always be sure whether an animal is just a variety of an existing species or is a distinct species in its own right.

Chapter 3, Struggle for Existence, explains that all species overreproduce. More are born than can survive, so they are in competition for resources. Darwin makes the point that the struggle for life is most severe between individuals and varieties of the same species. He gives examples of the complex relationships between plants and animals that occur in the environment.

Chapter 4, Natural Selection, compares natural and artificial selection and discusses sexual selection. Darwin was keen to emphasise that natural selection is a force that improves living things, even if it seems harsh when some species become extinct. He also explains divergence, where a single original form gives rise to descendants which become even more specialised.

Chapter 5, Laws of Variation, discusses Darwin's belief that something caused variations, but he did not know about genes and gene mutations. He believed variations were due to environmental factors acting on the reproductive process in some way. He also wrongly believed that the use or disuse of organs could lead directly to evolutionary change.

Chapter 6, Difficulties of the Theory, Darwin tries to avert criticism of the theory by discussing some of the main difficulties he realised people might have with his ideas. If species have descended from others why are there not numerous intermediate species in existence? Darwin's explanation is that the less specialised forms would have become extinct over time.

Another difficulty was that people found it difficult to believe that such a specialised creature as a bat could have evolved from another mammal. Darwin pointed out that there is evidence of intermediate forms between ground dwelling mammals and flying ones. 'Flying' squirrels exist that glide between treetops using a flap of skin formed between their front and rear legs. He also pointed out that among invertebrates there are varying degrees of complexity in the eye, showing stages in the development of sight.

Chapter 7, Objections to the Theory, was added to later editions in response to specific objections made by critics of the first edition. (These are examined in detail later in this chapter.)

Chapter 8, Instinct, Darwin believed animal behaviour could be explained by evolution; natural selection could work on instincts as well as physical appearance. He reasoned that if man could breed out the natural tendency of dogs to attack sheep then nature could behave in a similar way. Followers of Lamarck believed that instinct was a learned habit that eventually became inherited but Darwin points out that this cannot be the case in neuter insects such as bees and ants. He believed natural selection could work on families of insects as well as on individuals: even though some individuals are neuter and cannot reproduce they serve a useful purpose to the group as a whole.

Chapter 9, Hybridism, Darwin argues that the traditional view of what constitutes a species is incorrect. He shows that when species are very closely related they can crossbreed and some of the offspring may be fertile. This was in answer to critics who objected that species cannot be hybridised.

Chapter 10, The Imperfection of the Geological Record, discusses the imperfections in the fossil record as Darwin believed evolution must have taken place gradually but he knew the existing fossil record did not support this. There are periods when new species seem to suddenly come into existence without any intermediate forms before them. Darwin argued that fossil-bearing rocks are only laid down in certain circumstances so they don't show the complete history of the earth; also some may now be under oceans due to geological and climatic change.

Chapter 11, The Geological Succession of Organic Beings, argues that if we take into account the imperfections in the geological record then fossils support the theory of common descent. Intermediate forms of species had been found that link separate species like horses and pigs to a common ancestor.

Chapter 12, Geographical Distribution, shows the part that geographical factors play in the distribution of species. When parts of the world with similar conditions are compared they each have distinct species living there that are adapted to that specific environment. Ostriches in Africa, rheas in South America and emus in Australia all look superficially similar but they are totally separate species. When species are successful they spread out until they meet a natural barrier to migration such as an ocean. This means that each species will be characteristic of the environment in which it evolved.

Chapter 13, Geographical Distribution (continued), further examines geographical factors especially in relation to island habitats such as the Galapagos islands. The importance of ocean currents to migration is explained in relation to the ways in which islands become populated.

Chapter 14, Mutual Affinities of Organic Beings: Morphology: Embryology: Rudimentary Organs, again discusses the classification of species and puts forward the supporting evidence of the similarity between developing embryos of very different mammals and the significance of rudimentary organs as discussed in Chapter 4.

Chapter 15, Recapitulation and Conclusion, sums up the arguments of the previous chapters.

PUBLIC OUTRAGE

The *Origin of Species* was much more readable than other scientific theories and its controversial nature meant it was soon in the headlines. Darwin was careful not to spell out the fact that man was probably descended from apes and, indeed, avoided the question of human origins altogether in the book. Intelligent readers were able to work this out for themselves, however, and it threw the Christian world into uproar.

The chief objections of the Christian world to natural selection were:

* Darwin was denying divine creation – *The Bible* states that God created the world.

* Man was created in God's image and therefore could not be descended from apes.

Darwin's book was seen as blasphemous and the wife of the Bishop of Worcester spoke for many Christians when she said: 'Descended from the apes? My dear, let us hope that it is not true, but if it is, let us pray that it does not become generally known.' Cartoons of Darwin filled the papers and magazines, showing Darwin as part ape and part human. Darwin was even pointed out as 'the most dangerous man in Europe' by a clergyman who saw him while on a visit to the British

Museum. Even Darwin's old teacher at Cambridge, Adam Sedgwick, was greatly upset by his former pupil's 'error' and his turning away from religion. He thought the book was 'utterly false' and claimed it made him laugh until his sides ached.

Descended from apes??!!??

Christians often used the arguments presented by the Reverend William Paley in his *Evidences of Christianity* (1794) and *Natural Theology* (1802). Darwin himself had read these during his theological studies at Cambridge and at the time had been convinced by their logic. Paley believed each species was so well adapted to its environment that it must have been created by an intelligent creator; one who was benevolent and kind, who placed each creature in an environment where it would be happy.

The world of science had shown how each part of the body was perfectly formed to carry out the functions required. How could the mechanism of the eye, with its precise lens and adjustable pupil have been formed without a creator? This was the '**argument by design**' that many Christians used as proof against evolution. Paley reasoned that if someone had never seen a watch before its efficient mechanism must lead them to believe that it had been made by a creator. He argued that the natural world was the same. Even Charles Lyell, whose geological theories of change had been an inspiration to Darwin, used a similar argu-

KEYWORDS

Argument by design, name given to anti-Darwunian argument proposing that complex features could not have evolved but were designed by a creator.

Agnostic, person who believes the existence of God cannot be proved.

ment, giving the woodpecker as an example. He remarked on its strong skull that resisted pounding against trees, pointed beak to pick insects from tree bark; toes that gripped and pointed backwards – surely these features meant it had been created perfectly and any changes would make it less able to survive. But Lyell was open minded and prepared to be convinced by Darwin, unlike many of his contemporaries.

Eventually many Christians were able to reconcile their beliefs with the theory of evolution and believed that God intended the world to be created by natural means. The Reverend Charles Kingsley, the Queen's Chaplain, expressed this in a letter:'We know that God was so wise that he could make all things; but he is so much wiser even than that, that he can make all things make themselves.'

However, evolution was considered to be a mere hypothesis by the established Catholic Church until 1996, when it was eventually officially recognised by Pope John Paul II in a letter issued by the Vatican.

Darwin discusses his religious beliefs in his autobiography. While writing the *Origin of Species* he still believed in God but later he became an **agnostic**.

SCIENTIFIC DEBATE

In addition to the objections raised by religious believers there were also scientific arguments against the book. Some of the arguments were convincing enough for Darwin to question his belief in natural selection and later to amend the *Origin of Species*. However, discoveries made later, especially in the field of genetics, have led to the realisation that many ideas in Darwin's original version of the *Origin of Species* were correct but could not be explained by the science of the time.

Contemporary scientific objections

St George Mivart (1827–1900) was a geologist and at first he had accepted Darwin's theory of evolution but with some reservations; as a Catholic he believed that if evolution took place God had some part in it, perhaps providing the soul.

Eventually he became one of the chief objectors to the theory. His main argument was that natural selection couldn't explain the initial stages of well established adaptations. An eye or a wing is obviously a useful structure in its developed form but what selective advantage would it have in an undeveloped form? The book that outlined his theory, *On the Genesis of Species – to show that the Darwinian theory is untenable and that natural selection is not the Origin of Species*, was published in 1871.

Darwin argued in reply that these adaptations probably began with a different purpose from the one that they eventually ended up with. For example, feathers may have originally developed as a heat regulating mechanism which gave a natural advantage and developed their aerodynamic properties at a later stage of development.

Lord Kelvin (William Thomson, 1824–1907), a well-respected mathematician and physicist, objected to the theory on the grounds that the earth was not old enough for evolution to have taken place. He believed that the earth's interior had been hot since creation and must be constantly cooling. He took measurements and from his calculations he worked out that the earth was 20 million years old; older than Archbishop Ussher had calculated but not old enough for natural selection to have shaped living things.

Lord Kelvin was an expert on temperature and this evidence seemed incontrovertible at the time. His theory was later proved to be wrong when Pierre Curie discovered that radium salts give out heat. It was realised that radiation is responsible for maintaining the heat from the earth's crust, counteracting any cooling effect. Scientists are still debating the age of the earth – it could be nearly 5,000 million years old, which must be long enough for evolution to have taken place.

Sir Richard Owen (1804–1892) was an anatomist and zoologist who had worked with Darwin on the zoology of *The Beagle*. He wrote a scathing attack on the book in the *Edinburgh Review* which was published anonymously. He tried to discredit Darwin by twisting the facts and was probably motivated by professional jealousy.

Fleeming Jenkin (1833–1885), a Scottish engineer, dealt the biggest blow to Darwin's theory in 1867, when he suggested that any favourable advantage gained by an animal would be diluted when it bred with an animal without the advantage. Because the mechanism of inheritance was not understood it was thought that genetic factors were divisible or became 'watered down' or blended by breeding; any variations that came about would eventually diminish. This is now understood to be incorrect. Gregor Mendel, a Moravian monk, experimented on pea plants and discovered that there is no 'blending' of parental characteristics in the offspring. Although these experiments took place in the 1860s they were not widely known about until the twentieth century. (The relationship between genetics and evolution is discussed in more detail in the last chapter.)

At the time Darwin was writing he did not know of Mendel's experiments, and in 1868 he published a theory of **pangenesis** which attempted to explain the mechanism of inheritance as the result of particles or **gemmules**. He believed these gemmules acquired representative characteristics from all the organs and tissues of the adult body and they collected in the reproductive organs.

KEYWORDS

Pangenesis, Darwin's mistaken theory of genetic inheritance.

Gemmules, particles that Darwin erroneously thought were responsible for carrying genetic information.

During sexual reproduction the gemmules became mixed or reassorted in some way and this explained how different offspring of the same parents could resemble both parents to varying degrees. Darwin believed this explained the origin of variations. He also believed quite wrongly that some acquired characteristics gained during a lifetime could be inherited by the offspring and this theory helped him explain how it occurred.

Darwin's theory of pangenesis was totally incorrect but with the knowledge available at the time it seemed a completely logical explanation.

DARWIN'S SUPPORTERS

Darwin became very ill at the time of publication and spent some time taking the waters in Yorkshire. Although he saw the book as his chief argument for natural selection he needed friends to argue his case in the public scientific arena as he didn't have the physical strength to do it himself. Darwin's old friend Lyell supported his publication, but although he believed in evolution he was unsure about the mechanism of natural selection and believed God had some part in it. Darwin said he had him 'nearly converted'. The greatest of all Darwin's supporters was the distinguished zoologist, Thomas Henry Huxley (1825–1895). Huxley was so fierce in his support of the book that he became known as 'Darwin's bulldog'. On reading the *Origin of Species* he was immediately convinced by the argument and commented 'How stupid not to have thought of it before!'

Other early supporters were Joseph Hooker (1817–1911), a botanist who had helped to classify plant material from *The Beagle*; and John Lubbock (1834–1913). Lubbock lived near Down House and had been greatly influenced by Darwin as a young man. Other scientists also lent their support – Asa Gray, an American botanist, was instrumental in supporting Darwin in the United States.

The biggest public debate took place in Oxford in June 1860, when Darwin's supporters, Huxley and Hooker, confronted the Bishop of Oxford, Samuel Wilberforce, at a meeting of the British Association for the Advancement of Science. The meeting was chaired by John Henslow, Darwin's old friend and teacher. He did not agree with Darwin's theory but believed he should get a fair hearing.

On the second day of the meeting Huxley felt overwhelmed by the strength of feeling against Darwin and believed people were not prepared to listen objectively. He was about to leave when by chance he bumped into Robert Chambers, the author of *Vestiges of the Natural History of Creation*. Chambers convinced Huxley that he should stay and fight the cause of evolution.

On the third day the meeting was moved into the University Museum Library because of the numbers who wanted to attend. Over 700 people crammed themselves into the hall to listen to this important debate.

The Bishop enraged Darwin's side by asking Huxley if he was descended from an ape on his grandmother's or grandfather's side of the family. The Bishop was a very persuasive speaker, earning him the nickname of 'Soapy Sam'. He had been primed beforehand by Owen on scientific questions and was supported by other speakers – even FitzRoy came forward to argue against Darwin. He was now an admiral and still a staunch Christian.

Although Huxley put forward good arguments on Darwin's behalf he was not an inspiring speaker. It was Hooker who managed to save the day for Darwin. Afterwards he wrote to Darwin explaining how he demonstrated that Wilberforce was 'ignorant about the rudiments of botanical science'. When questioned it was obvious that Wilberforce had never even read the book in question. 'Sam was shut up – had not one word to say in reply, and the meeting was dissolved forthwith.'

PUBLIC ACCEPTANCE
By the end of the 1860s most scientists had come to accept the idea of evolution. Not all of them understood the theory of natural selection, or accepted it. Many still believed that the ideas of Lamarck were correct: characteristics acquired by parents in their lifetime would be

inherited by their offspring. Even Darwin modified his theories to take account of this belief. Many also believed that if evolution existed it was part of God's plan and that man still had a special place in the world and had intellect by divine right. Darwin did not make the theory that man had evolved from ape-like creatures explicit in the *Origin of Species*. He said, rather cryptically: 'Light will be thrown on the origins of Man and his history.' Then he began working on a new book to try to address the question of human origins – *The Descent of Man*.

✳ ✳ ✳ ✳ SUMMARY ✳ ✳ ✳ ✳

- Darwin was virtually forced into publishing the *Origin of Species* after receiving a paper from Alfred Russel Wallace in 1858.

- The book was published in 1859, was an instant success and is still in print today.

- Several editions of the book were produced, the one generally available today is the 6th edition containing 15 chapters.

- The book caused public outrage and indignation, especially among Christians.

- Scientific objections came from St George Mivart, Lord Kelvin, Sir Richard Owen and Fleeming Jenkin, among others.

- Darwin's main supporters were Thomas Huxley, John Lubbock and Joseph Hooker.

- Darwin was unable to answer some of the main objections to his theory because he did not understand genetics.

6 Darwin's Later Years

Darwin became a public figure after the publication of the *Origin of Species*. He found this celebrity difficult to cope with and his health became worse, so much so that he hardly left the house. In addition to the water cures he had been taking he tried various diets, and ice packs applied to the spine, which were supposed to shock the circulation. Some of the cures worked for a short time but nothing gave him permanent relief. He was a great worrier which didn't help matters: he worried about his finances, although he had a great deal of money and the accounts were in the capable hands of his wife Emma; he was also worried about the health of his children, believing they had inherited weaknesses from him. He found the verbal attacks of his opponents stressful and suffered as a result of the pressure of his work. Perhaps his illness gave him a good excuse for refusing to see people and for resting his active mind.

He still tried to work every day at home leaving public speaking to his followers; Huxley was his foremost champion. 'Darwinist' was the popular term for those who followed the increasingly popular creed of 'Darwinism'. Many young radicals and scientists wanted to break away from the orthodox beliefs of the church and saw Darwin as their hero. Many of these followers did not understand the details of the theory of evolution but they believed that the *Origin of Species* gave a scientific basis for overthrowing the old order. Huxley was extremely interested in the idea that humans have apes as ancestors and was a popular speaker at working men's groups. Demand for information on the subject was overwhelming – 2,000 people were turned away from one of Huxley's London lectures in 1866.

The theory of evolution gradually became acceptable to the public and Huxley wrote to Darwin in 1868: 'You will have the rare happiness to see your ideas triumphant during your lifetime.' A cheaper edition of the *Origin of Species* was made available as an experiment to see if it would be bought by workers and the less well off; it sold out very quickly.

His achievements eventually became recognised by the academic world. In 1864 he was given the Copley Medal, the highest honour of the Royal Society, and in 1877 he was given an honorary doctorate from the University of Cambridge.

A BUSY LIFE

Darwin disliked all this public attention. He was often asked to endorse the views of **atheists**, which made him particularly distressed, mainly because of his wife's belief in Christianity. He wrote in reply to one of these enquiries from Edward Aveling in 1880:

> **KEYWORD**
>
> Atheists, people who believe God does not exist.

> It appears to me (whether rightly or wrongly) that direct arguments against Christianity & theism produce hardly any effect on the public; & freedom of thought is best promoted by the gradual illumination of men's minds, which follows from the advance of science. It has therefore been always my object to avoid writing on religion, & I have confined myself to science. I may however have been unduly biased by the pain which it would give some members of my family, if I aided in any way direct attacks on religion.

Darwin wished to stay at home quietly and concentrate on his many experiments, although his body was weak his mind was keen and sharp and he was constantly getting new ideas about experiments he could do that would confirm the ideas in the *Origin of Species*. In addition to this work he carried out a vast correspondence with people who had read his books, friends, acquaintances and scientific contacts as well as sending out lists of questions to people who bred pigeons or orchids, farmers, collectors, travellers; in fact anyone whom he thought might be able to give him information. As the Darwin family kept most of their correspondence it can still be studied today.

He also read, or had his wife read to him, many current works including those written by scientists who opposed him and religious and moral objectors to his books. Because the term 'survival of the fittest' became popular, his theory was often misrepresented by those who wished to justify the class distinctions in Victorian society. They believed that the poor were at the bottom of society because they deserved to be there, they were not 'fit' enough to be at the top. Darwin was often verbally attacked by social reformers who believed these views to be his own.

In contrast, he was also congratulated by those who wished to see a **secular** society, Karl Marx sent him a copy of *Das Kapital* inscribed 'from a sincere admirer'. Marx wanted to see a more equal society and believed that religion was one of the factors that kept workers oppressed. It was not surprising that Darwin wanted to keep away from public debate for, on the one hand, he was being accused of trying to overthrow religion, morals and society and, on the other, he was accused of supporting a rigid hierarchical social system!

> **KEYWORD**
>
> Secular, non-religious.

Darwin spent time helping the local community: on the school board and at the local magistrates' court. He was involved with the running of

Darwin under pressure of work.

the local parish church, a fact which may surprise those who view him as some kind of anti-religious figure. He became involved with charity work, too, sending money to enable a new variety of potato to be developed which was resistant to blight. A terrible famine had occurred in Ireland as a result of this disease and Darwin hoped it could be wiped out by judicious plant breeding. In addition to this work he was still revising the *Origin of Species* and working on new books – no wonder he felt ill and stressed at times!

PUBLICATIONS AFTER THE ORIGIN OF SPECIES

The books and articles that he wrote after *Origin* continued the themes he had worked on for most of his life. Everything he wrote was connected in some way to the question of evolution. He did not concentrate on trying to trace the line of man from his animal origins because he felt there was not enough fossil evidence to be able to make connections and follow a line of development. Instead he concentrated on looking at tiny details that would give evidence to show the ways in which natural selection worked. Because of this, many of his publications are only of real interest to a small number of specialists, although some of them, for example the *Descent of Man*, were very popular at the time and are still in print today.

On the Various Contrivances by which British and Foreign Orchids are Fertilised by Insects, and on the Good Effects of Intercrossing

This was published in May 1862 as a result of many years of experimentation at Down House. Darwin had become interested in the intricate colours and shapes of orchids while on holiday in Devon. Wealthy Victorians were passionate about collecting rare and unusual orchids and had them sent from overseas. Darwin wrote to many of them for specimens and also obtained some from Kew Gardens. His main interest was in the fertilisation process, for without sexual reproduction there would be no variations among plants, and transmutation could not occur. Many species of orchid have elaborate petals with curious shapes that mimic those of insects. Darwin wanted to show that this is a means of getting insects to transfer **pollen** from one to the other and ensuring crossfertilisation. Eventually he had to set up his own hothouse at Down where he imitated the action of pollinating insects with

a paintbrush. Darwin believed that because the British bee orchid was self-pollinated it would eventually become extinct. It is now an extremely rare plant.

Darwin was one of the first people to observe and explain the pollination of plants and one of the first to do very detailed examinations and descriptions of plant anatomy. He showed that complex flowers could have been produced by evolution because there were less developed species in existence which looked as if their forms were leading up to the more complex ones. He showed that insects had developed to match the structure of the flowers because it was important for them to obtain nectar.

Although the book was not a bestseller it was well received by botanists and was important because it showed more evidence in support of evolution. In the introduction he wrote: 'In my volume on the Origin of Species I have given only general reasons for my belief that it is apparently a universal law of nature that organic beings require an occasional cross with another individual … I wish to show that I have not spoken without having gone into details.' It was this attention to detailed evidence which led to Darwin's theory of evolution being generally accepted.

On the Movements and Habits of Climbing Plants, The Power of Movement in Plants

On the Movements and Habits of Climbing Plants (1865) and *The Power of Movement in Plants* (1880) were books on similar subjects that came about as a result of a paper Darwin received from Asa Gray in 1858. This concerned the climbing tendrils of pumpkin plants. Darwin became curious about climbing plants and did his own experiments on them with assistance from his son, Francis.

He came to the conclusion that different environmental stimuli produced different movements in stems, roots , leaves, etc. These movements were generally spiral in nature. The hypothesis that he drew from this was that there was some substance in the roots and tips of the plants which controlled the bending process. Darwin was ahead of his time for it was the first experimental evidence that showed the existence of plant hormones which were not isolated until the 1930s.

The Variation of Animals and Plants under Domestication

The years after the publication of *Origin*, from 1859 until 1866, were mostly taken up with work on this book, which was developed from research not used in the *Origin of Species*. It was published in January 1868 in two volumes. Darwin believed it to be one of his more important works but little reference is made to it today.

Artificial selection is discussed in the *Origin of Species* but Darwin had a great quantity of material on this subject which could not be fitted into the finished book. In 1839 he had sent out a questionnaire on stock breeding to numerous farmers and animal breeders. He used their replies as a basis for *The Variation ... under Domestication* and included his own research on pigeons where he describes fully 'all the chief races, their history, the amount and nature of their differences and the probable steps by which they have been formed'. There are also chapters on other subjects for intensive breeding, for example goldfish, cereals, and honey bees.

The second volume of the book concerns Darwin's theory of pangenesis which was his attempt to explain heredity before **genes** or **chromosomes** had been discovered. (This is discussed in more detail in Chapter 7.) Although the theory was completely wrong it was an ingenious solution to a problem that no one else had been able to solve at the time.

KEYWORDS

Genes, small indivisible units of heredity.

Chromosomes, thread-like structures within a cell that carry genes.

The Descent of Man and Selection in Relation to Sex

This book, published in 1871, was the work hinted at in the *Origin of Species* by the sentence 'Light will be thrown on the origin of Man and his history.' It linked man to animal ancestors and discussed religion and morals but by this time Darwin's ideas were not new and the book caused much less controversy than *Origin*. The book consists of two parts: Part One explores man's descent from ape-like creatures and Part Two discusses sexual selection, the concluding chapters linking together the two strands.

Part One

The first part of the book used the available evidence from embryology, anatomy and behavioural studies to show that there were many physical similarities between humans and apes. It also showed ways in which instinct and emotions were similar. But although there are many similarities people have a much bigger brain capacity than apes and have developed civilisation. Darwin thought that there must have been some unique factors that led to development of the human brain, perhaps due to environmental conditions.

His explanation was that the upright posture of mankind and the ability to walk on two legs led us out of the forests and allowed us to use our hands. This led to the development of the brain. In this he was partly correct, for fossils have been discovered that indicate that the earliest humans stood upright before brains had developed.

Readers today will find *The Descent of Man* a racist book because Darwin believed, like most of his contemporaries, that white people were mentally superior to black 'savages'. Some anthropologists even believed that societies of 'savages' were at an earlier stage of evolution than western societies. This was a popular view because it justified the exploitation of the world by industrialised nations as the 'survival of the fittest'.

Part Two

Although Darwin had come to the conclusion that all races of mankind shared the same ancestors he could not explain how certain racial features could be explained by adaptation. He decided that sexual selection had a part to play and he collected evidence from animals, birds and insects to show the way that this worked in nature.

He also sent out a questionnaire to his many correspondents around the world for information on the idea of beauty among different races. He concluded that any non-adaptive characteristics that distinguished the different races were as a result of their differing perceptions of beauty in a potential mate.

The Expression of the Emotions in Man and Animals

This book, published in 1872, was one of the first to contain photographs, which made it rather expensive at the time, but in spite of that it sold very well. Darwin became interested in the way emotions were expressed when his son William was born. He kept meticulous records of his son's behaviour and this led him to wonder if the expression of behaviour was learned or whether it was inherited in some way.

He again sent out questionnaires to his contacts, this time a sheet of 16 questions concerning emotional behaviour. He wanted to investigate whether different races use the same gestures or use the same facial expressions when they feel emotions such as shame or fear or joy. Could animals be said to feel and show emotions? The results were intended to be included as a chapter in the *Descent of Man* but as there was so much information Darwin decided to devote a whole book to the subject.

Darwin came to the conclusion that humans share many behavioural expressions with other animals, and linked this with his belief in human animal origins; for example a sneer, where the lip is curled, might have developed from a snarl. The only human emotional response he could not find in animals was blushing.

Darwin was a pioneer in observation of animal behaviour, and some scientists today are not only working on emotional responses in animals but are trying to determine whether or not they possess consciousness. This book again shows the unique way in which Darwin's mind worked; again he observed things that anyone could have observed, he made connections and drew conclusions that anyone could have done, but nobody had thought of doing it.

Insectivorous plants

Published in 1875, this book was again written as a result of Darwin's observations while on holiday. He could never go anywhere without studying the natural world around him and once his curiosity was aroused he was deter-mined to carry out experiments to satisfy it. In

KEYWORDS

Insectivorous, animal or plant that feeds on insects.

Physiology, study of the way living things function.

1860 he was in the Sussex countryside with the family when he saw a variety of sundew, an **insectivorous** plant. He realised that he knew very little about such plants and wanted to find out more, so he stud-ied sundews, Venus flytraps and bladderworts. The **physiology** of the plants really interested him and he did experiments on the types of food they would eat, feeding them on a variety of substances: milk, urine, saliva, alcohol, strong tea, roast beef, vegetables and hard boiled egg. He also tried poisons: strychnine, quinine, nicotine, morphine and snake venom.

Although some of the experiments were somewhat frivolous, Darwin realised that the plants had become insect eaters as an adaptation to supply themselves with nitrogen which was missing in the poor soils in which they grew. Another small detail was added to the understanding of plant evolution.

The Effects of Cross and Self-Fertilisation in the Vegetable Kingdom, The Different Forms of Flowers and Plants of the Same Species

These books, published in 1876 and 1877 respectively, continued the detailed work on the fertilisation of plants that had always fascinated

Darwin. By chance he observed two beds of Linaria vulgaris in the 1830's. One bed of the plants had been crossfertilised and one had self-fertilised. The crossed plants seemed to be more vigorous. He observed and experimented on this subject for 11 years and found that where there was close interbreeding among plants fewer seeds were produced than among plants that were crossed with another plant. Darwin believed that in order to be strong most plants had evolved mechanisms to eliminate self-fertilisation.

Some plants are self-pollinating, a trait that would have evolutionary value where they were trying to take over new habitat. If they were the only plants there they would have to self-pollinate and they could spread rapidly and colonise the area. This is only a good strategy in the short term because there is less variation among self-pollinated plants. If there were any changes in the environment these plants would be less likely to evolve adaptations than crosspollinated plants. Darwin then became interested in plants such as the primrose which have more than one type of flower. He believed this was also a phenomenon linked to crossfertilisation.

Neither of the books was a public success but Darwin believed that *The Different Forms of Flowers and Plants* had given him the greatest pleasure to work on. The experimental methods he devised while working on the two books are still in use by plant biologists today.

The Formation of Vegetable Mould, through the Action of Worms, with Observations on Their Habits

This book of 1881 was Darwin's last publication before he died. He had always been interested in worms and the way in which they formed the soil that was necessary for plant growth. When visiting Maer as a young man he had been fascinated by the worm casts pointed out by his uncle; later, in 1877, he was present at an archaeological dig of a Roman villa and realised it was probably the actions of worms over the years that had buried it.

Darwin got his family to work and they carried out a series of experiments at Down. An ingenious wormstone was devised and placed in the garden where it sank into the ground over the years. The rate of sinking was measured by a central gauge and the amount of soil that the worms brought up could be calculated from this. Darwin visited Stonehenge to observe the depth of soil around the fallen stones there.

The worms were also subjected to other experiments: they were not sensitive to the sound of whistles, shouting, bassoon playing or the piano but they did react to vibration when placed on the piano. There were experiments with coloured lanterns, candles and paraffin lamps and their sense of smell was tested with perfume and tobacco smoke. What and how they ate was observed as well as the way in which they dragged leaves into their burrows.

This book was very popular at the time for it was easy to read and it seemed that everyone knew something about the subject and had their own observations to add. It led to a huge amount of correspondence that totally swamped the Darwin family.

Autobiography of Charles Darwin

Darwin's autobiography was begun in May 1876, not long after he found out he was to be a grandfather for the first time. It was intended for the family and was a fairly honest account of his life when compared to other autobiographies of the time. After his death it was revised by his son Francis and made public in 1892.

THE FINAL YEARS

Darwin continued writing and working right until the end of his life and, although his health had its ups and downs, he did not seem to be getting any worse. His son Francis helped him with some of his experimental work and his daughter Henrietta became his secretary. He still kept to his daily routine and worked hard long after most people had retired.

In December 1881 he had a mild heart attack and later, in April 1882, he suffered from a more severe attack which led to his death on 19 April, aged 73. His family was by his side. Some people would like to believe that Darwin had a deathbed conversion to Christianity but this story is not true.

The family wanted him to be buried in the local church but were persuaded by John Lubbock that he should be buried at Westminster Abbey with full public honours. He was laid to rest near another famous scientist, Sir Isaac Newton.

＊＊＊＊SUMMARY＊＊＊＊

- Darwin did not enjoy the celebrity that his work brought him and continued to work quietly at home.

- Radicals and atheists believed his book supported the formation of a secular society.

- Social reformers believed his book supported the established hierarchical system.

- Darwin wrote many books after the *Origin of Species* and they were all connected with evolution to some extent. None was as controversial as the *Origin of Species*, even the *Descent of Man* which discussed how humans had developed from ape-like creatures.

- He died in April 1882 aged 73, and was buried at Westminster Abbey.

Beyond Darwin

The theory of evolution was generally accepted after Darwin's death and most people began to come to terms with the ideas in the *Origin of Species* although there were still some Christians who could not accept any ideas that were in opposition to *The Bible*. In social terms Darwinism became popular due to the mistaken belief that 'survival of the fittest' was a term that applied to human society, a belief that became known as Social Darwinism

SOCIAL DARWINISM

Those who believed that Darwin's ideas could be applied to human society became known as Social Darwinists. This belief was popularised by Herbert Spencer (1820–1903) who believed that economic competition should be encouraged to make society stronger. In a capitalist society those with the most money are seen as the most successful. In Spencer's terms millionaires must be the fittest in society and the poor are the weakest. He believed, in the same way that Malthus did, that if the poor multiplied beyond their means they would die out, as they had during the Irish potato famine. This was natural selection at work on a human scale. These ideas were widely read in the late Victorian era for they tied in with the theory of 'self-help' proposed by Samuel Smiles in his popular book of the same title published in 1859. In his view hard work paid off and the poor had only themselves to blame for any hardship they suffered, now natural history seemed to support the view that the superior would triumph. Social Darwinists believed that natural selection justified not giving aid to the poor as it went against the natural order.

These ideas were taken to their logical but awful conclusion by Francis Galton (1822–1911), in a book written in 1869, *Hereditary Genius*. He believed that heredity was the most important part of the natural selection process and he showed how intelligence was passed down through families. He thought that society should breed only from the most superior individuals in the same way that farmers breed from their best stock. Humans should be artificially selected by encouraging 'superior' people to have children. Furthermore, he thought that poor, slum dwelling families should be prevented from producing offspring by means of compulsory birth control. Anyone with physical or mental disabilities should be

KEYWORDS

Eugenics, 'Improving' racial qualities by controlling inherited characteristics.

Abiogenesis, spontaneous generation of living things.

institutionalised and not allowed to breed. This policy was known as **eugenics** and it became popular at the beginning of the twenieth century. It was taken to gross extremes in Nazi Germany where wholesale extermination of 'undesirables' took place in an effort to create the master race. Darwin cannot be blamed for such genocide even though some of its followers were inspired by his books.

NEO-DARWINISM

Although the idea of evolution became popular in social and scientific terms the mechanism of natural selection fell out of favour in the scientific world because nobody could convincingly explain how the characteristics of parents were inherited by their offspring. Darwin's explanation of pangenesis and gemmules was obviously flawed. Even he had conceded, wrongly, that Lamarck might have been correct in believing that characteristics acquired during an animal's lifetime in response to environmental factors could be passed on to the next generation. So although evolution became an acceptable idea, natural selection did not and Lamarckism came into favour, even among many of Darwin's followers.

Scientists who remained true to the idea of natural selection and opposed to the belief that acquired characteristics could be inherited became known as Neo-Darwinists. The process of inheritance was still inexplicable for the life process itself was poorly understood. Many ordinary people still believed that living things could be born out of inanimate matter, for it was only in the 1860s that Louis Pasteur (1822–1895) proved that there was no such thing as **abiogenesis**.

Living things can only come from living things and cannot be the products of spontaneous generation.

Although many scientific discoveries were made during the nineteenth century scientific equipment was sometimes primitive by today's standards. Investigations at cell level could not

KEYWORD

Cytology, study of cells.

be made, for microscopes were not capable of examining many of the complex structures within cells. It was not until the end of the nineteenth century, when microscopes became more powerful, that the science of **cytology** was developed. August Weissman, a German naturalist, was able to identify the nucleus of the germ cell as the carrier of genetic information in 1885, as a result of these scientific advances.

Weissman, a Neo-Darwinist, experimented for many years trying to prove that acquired characteristics could not be inherited. He cut the tails off generations of rats but didn't find one case where the offspring

Are muscles inherited?

were born without tails as a result of their parents' experiences. He could find no evidence that the muscles of manual workers were passed on to their children, or that any scars or mutilations were inherited. He concluded that some kind of 'germ plasm' existed in the reproductive cell nucleus of both parents which was not influenced by any changes that occurred to other cells in the body. When the sperm penetrates the ovum during reproduction equal contributions are made by both parents to the inherited characteristics within the fertilised egg. There is no blending or diluting of characteristics.

By the end of the nineteenth century, as more advances were made in observing the minute details within the cell nucleus, it was thought that thread like structures called chromosomes probably carried this genetic information. It was not until 1953 when the structure of **DNA**

KEYWORD

DNA, deoxyribonucleic acid. Molecule that forms the genetic material of living things.

was discovered that this genetic information was fully understood.

THE BIRTH OF GENETICS

Weissman's discoveries tied in with research that had been rediscovered at the beginning of the twentieth century. In the 1860s, during Darwin's lifetime, Gregor Mendel (1822–1884), a Moravian monk, had been working on the problem of inherited characteristics. There is some evidence to suggest that the journal containing Mendel's research was among Darwin's papers but there is no evidence to show that he had read it, for it was not marked in any way and Darwin usually made notes on everything he read. But even if Darwin had read the paper it is unlikely that he would have understood its implications for it was based on mathematical theory and Darwin had always been a poor mathematician. Mendel's work was largely ignored during his lifetime and he did not belong to the scientific circle based in London so it is unlikely that Darwin could have made any connections between their work.

Mendel wished to improve crop yields at the monastery so he started on a programme of crop breeding experiments. Instead of looking at the whole plant he concentrated on looking at single characteristics. He believed that there must be some logical structure to the mechanism of inheritance so he chose plants that differed from each other unmistakably in an either/or way. He chose peas that were either tall or short, had green seeds or yellow, had wrinkled seeds or unwrinkled. These were easily distinguishable for the purpose of his experiment and meant that his calculations did not have to be too complicated.

In one example of his experiments he chose a strain of tall peas that was pure, in other words when the peas self-fertilised they always produced tall offspring. He crossed these with a pure strain of dwarf peas. The resulting **hybrid**

KEYWORD

Hybrid, crossbred plant or animal.

generation of peas were all tall. However, when the hybrids were interbred he obtained a mixed crop of tall and dwarf peas in a ratio of 3:1. When he did a similar experiment with peas that bore either yellow or green peas he obtained a first generation of peas that were all yellow. The yellow hybrids then produced a second generation of yellow and green peas in a ratio of 3:1 again. The experiments were carried out many times with many types of peas and the results were always the same. There was no blending of characteristics, there were no in-between colours and heights of peas. They were either tall or dwarf but not medium sized, yellow or green but not a greeny-yellow.

Had Darwin known of these experiments it would have given him an argument to use against Fleeming Jenkin who argued that natural selection could not take place because any favourable adaptations would be lost or diluted by breeding. Mendel had shown that this was not the case, genetic material was indivisible. Mendel also showed that characteristics of a plant could appear to vanish but could then reappear in the next generation. This was also important for it demonstrated that the appearance of any living thing was not necessarily a guide to its genetic structure. A yellow pea could contain both green and yellow genetic material. In order to trace the line of descent of any creature it is important to look at more than its surface appearance –

you need to look inside the cells themselves. This was only really possible after Darwin's death.

The rediscovery of Mendel's work should have led to the theory of natural selection being finally accepted by the scientific community, for this evidence, taken in conjunction with that of Weissman, sounded the death knell for Lamarckism. However, although it was seen

KEYWORD

Mutation, genetic change that can give rise to inherited characteristics.

that Lamarck's theory was incorrect, new objections to natural selection were made on the basis of genetic **mutations**.

MUTATIONS OR STEADY STATE?

Darwin had always stressed that evolution was a slow and gradual process, that it progressed by the means of imperceptible novelties. The geneticists who discovered Mendel's work were misled into believing that evolution must take place in a series of jumps or 'saltations' for they believed that abrupt mutations were the cause of new characteristics being developed. Mendel had simplified his experiments and had only worked on plants. Both these factors meant that the complex features of animal and human inheritance were not taken into account. There was a vigorous debate for about 30 years between laboratory-based geneticists, who believed in evolution through mutation, and Neo-Darwinists, who studied the evolution of populations in the wild and believed in slow and steady evolutionary development.

By 1930 it was finally realised that large mutations are harmful and in any case they are fairly rare. R.A. Fisher and J.B.S. Haldane studied genetic factors in large populations and realised that many small mutations had previously been overlooked. Eventually the two opposing sides came together in a type of Darwinism that has come to be known as the 'New Synthesis'.

Today most scientists agree that this synthesis between genetics and Darwinism is the explanation for an open ended and divergent process of evolution. Analysis of DNA and proteins mean that relationships between species can be investigated, and these investigations tend to support Darwin, but there are still some questions to be answered. One of the more recent controversies was that of 'punctuated equilibria' put forward by N. Eldredge and S.J. Gould. They pointed out that new species seem to appear suddenly in the fossil record. Opponents point to the fact that suddenness in geological time may be thousands of years in ordinary time – so the scientific debate continues. Most of the more recent arguments against Darwin have been on religious grounds, for creationism has made a comeback.

RELIGION AGAINST SCIENCE

There has always been a clash between those who try to explain the way the world works in scientific terms and those who would prefer to see the world as the work of a creator that should be taken on faith. When European society was a religious one people could be put to death for believing that the earth went round the sun, for the earth was seen as the centre of God's creation.

Today our world is largely a secular one and in democratic nations there is freedom of speech – you can stand up in public and say the sun goes round the earth if you want to. Everyone has the right to put forward any theory they wish to, but in order for a theory to be considered a scientific truth there must be supporting evidence.

Darwin caused controversy when he put forward the theory of evolution but over the next century there was enough scientific proof for most people to accept that what he had said was correct. However, there are still people with strong religious beliefs who cannot accept the theory and creationism is becoming more popular, especially among fundamentalist Christians.

In Britain the Evolution Protest Movement was started in 1932. This group was determined to prove that evolution could not be a scientific fact and show that it is in opposition to biblical teaching. But it is in the United States that creationism really took hold. In 1925 the state of Tennessee banned anyone teaching the theory that man had descended from animals. Things came to a head when a teacher, John Scopes, was put on trial for teaching the theory of evolution. The trial attracted a great deal of publicity which led 20 other states to debate anti-evolution laws. Eventually it was decided that evolution could be taught in schools, except in Arkansas and Mississippi. Despite the fact that scientists seemed to have won the day for evolution the controversy surrounding the trials led to the disappearance of any mention of the theory in school textbooks until the 1950s.

The controversy that led to the modern rise in creationism began with the publication of *The Genesis Flood* in 1961. Written by Henry Morris and John Whitcomb, this book was an attempt to give evidence to support the fact that the book of Genesis was literally true. The book claims to give evidence that the world was formed in literally six days, less than 10,000 years ago, fossils and large geological formations were produced during Noah's flood, facts that are not supported by current scientific thinking. The authors also believe limited natural selection may take place, for example, the two dogs taken on board the ark may have given rise to all types of living dog, according to God's plan.

The book became a best seller and was the beginning of the 'creation science' movement which led to the formation of the Institute for Creation Research in 1972; a chain of events that started controversy in the United States education system yet again. If creationism is a science then it can be taught in state schools, which are not allowed to teach religious beliefs according to the American constitution. Schools in some religious areas of the country maintained that equal time should be given to teaching creation science and evolution, causing a dilemma for many teachers. This was resolved by a Supreme Court decision in 1987 ruling that 'creation science' is really a religious belief and not a true science.

Creationists are still a powerful lobby group, particularly in some of the American 'Bible Belt' states, although the phenomenon is spreading throughout the world. It is a belief that is not confined only to

Christians, for Islamic creationist groups have also been set up. The controversy continues with books such as Phillip Johnson's *Darwin on Trial*, which puts forward evidence against Darwin, and Kenneth Miller's *Finding Darwin's God*, which examines the creationists objections to evolution and shows where scientific research has disproved them.

There can be no real conclusion to this debate for scientific explanations only concern the material world and not the spiritual one. Although Darwin is still at the centre of the debate between religion and science, a position he never wanted to occupy, he continues to be remembered and honoured today because his ideas have stood the tests of scientific scrutiny over time.

✵ ✵ ✵ ✵SUMMARY✵ ✵ ✵ ✵

- Natural selection was used as an excuse not to aid the poor. This was known as Social Darwinism.

- Eugenics developed from this, its aim to improve racial qualities by selective breeding.

- Natural selection fell out of favour with many scientists, even those who believed evolution occurred.

- Mendel's early discoveries on inheritance could have been used to support Darwin's theories, had anyone known about them.

- Neo-Darwinists were those who supported Darwin's views long after he had died.

- Support for Darwin came from August Weissman who investigated whether acquired characteristics could be inherited.

- Some scientists believed abrupt genetic mutations were responsible for evolution but by the 1930s this was proved incorrect.

- The 'new synthesis' takes into account genetic factors; evidence from DNA tends to support Darwin.

- Objections to Darwin's theory are now chiefly by 'creation scientists'.

Glossary

Abiogenesis
Spontaneous generation of living things.

Agnostic
Person who believes the existence of God cannot be proved.

Archaeopteryx
Primitive, part reptilian bird.

Argument by design
Name given to anti-Darwinian argument proposing that complex features could not have evolved but were designed by a creator.

Artificial selection
Selection of animals or plants by breeders in order to develop desired characteristics in the offspring.

Atheists
People who believe God does not exist.

Atrophied
Wasted away.

Botany
The study of plant biology.

Catastrophism
Geological theory proposing that the earth's crust was shaped by violent events.

Chromosomes
Thread-like structures within a cell that carry genes.

Chronometers
Very accurate ships' clocks used to compare local and Greenwich time, thus establishing longitude.

Creationist
Theory that the world was created not by random events but by divine intervention.

Cytology
Study of cells.

DNA
Deoxyribonucleic acid. Molecule that forms the genetic material of living things.

Eugenics
'Improving' racial qualities by controlling inherited characteristics.

Evolution
Development of species from earlier forms.

Fossils
Ancient remains of plants and animals hardened into rock.

Gauchos
South American cowboys.

Gemmules
Particles that Darwin erroneously thought were responsible for carrying genetic information.

Genes
Small indivisible units of heredity.

Genetics
Study of heredity and variation.

Geology
The scientific study of the earth's crust.

Hybrid
Crossbred plant or animal.

Industrial Revolution
Period of history when trade and industry progressed rapidly due to technological progress.

Insectivorous
Animal or plant that feeds on insects.

Invertebrates
Creatures without backbones.

Longitude
Angular measurement of how far east or west a place is from the Greenwich Meridian in London.

Materialist
One who believes that all ideas and beliefs are a result of the material world and not the result of divine intervention.

Mutation
Genetic change that can give rise to inherited characteristics.

Natural selection
Theory that natural processes cause the survival of living things best suited to their environment.

Naturalist
Student of animals and plants.

Palaeontology
Study of life in the distant geological past, usually from fossil remains.

Pangenesis
Darwin's mistaken theory of genetic inheritance.

Philologist
Student of language.

Physiognomy
Method of judging a person's character by the shape and size of their facial features.

Physiology
Study of the way living things function.

Pollen
The fertilising powder of a plant.

Progressionism
Theory proposing that the world was created in a series of stages.

Radical
A person who wants fundamental changes in political systems and society.

Rudimentary
Undeveloped part or organ.

Secular
Non-religious.

Species
A group of similar plants and animals that are able to produce fertile offspring.

Strata
Layers in rock formations.

Survival of the fittest
A phrase invented by Herbert Spencer (1820–1903). In the struggle for survival the fittest will live to reproduce.

The Beagle
Survey ship that Darwin joined in a round the world voyage.

Transmutation
Change in the form or structure of a species over time.

Unitarians
Believers in a form of Christianity that sees God as an individual and not a trinity.

CHRONOLOGY OF MAJOR EVENTS IN DARWIN'S LIFE

1809 Born on 12 February in Shrewsbury, England.

1818 Enters Shrewsbury School.

1825 Attends Edinburgh University to study medicine.

1827 Enters Christ's College Cambridge to study for the ministry.

1831 Receives BA from Cambridge.

Joins crew of *The Beagle* in voyage around the world.

1836 Returns to England.

1837 Begins transmutation notebooks.

1839 Marries cousin, Emma Wedgwood.

Voyage of the Beagle published.

1859 *On the Origin of Species* published.

1871 *The Descent of Man* published.

1872 *The Expression of Emotion in Man and Animals* published.

1882 Dies at Down House on 19 April and buried at Westminster Abbey on 25 April.

FURTHER READING

WORKS BY CHARLES DARWIN

Many versions of the *Origin of Species* are available, generally the 6th edition. The best value is probably:

* *The Origin of Species*, Jeff Wallace (ed.), Wordsworth Editions Ltd, 1998.

* *On the Origin of Species*, Harvard University Press, 1975. The complete 1st edition with an excellent introduction.

* *The Voyage of the Beagle*. An excellent value version is available from Wordsworth Editions Ltd, 1997.

* *The Expression of Emotions in Man and Animals*, Paul Elkman (ed.), Fontana Press, 1999.

* *The Descent of Man*, H. James Birx (ed.), Prometheus Books, 1997.

* *The Portable Darwin*, Duncan H. Porter and Peter W. Graham, Penguin, 1993. Extracts from many of Darwin's works including the more obscure ones with introductory notes for each section.

WORKS ON DARWIN AND EVOLUTION

* *The Life of Charles Darwin*, Francis Darwin, Senate, 1995. First published in 1902, this is his son's account of his life and includes Darwin's autobiography.

* *Darwin*, Adrian Desmond and James Moore, Penguin, 1992. Fascinating and full of detail regarding Darwin's private life.

* *Charles Darwin – the Man and his Influence*, Peter J. Bowler, Cambridge University Press, 2000. Interesting evaluation of Darwin as a product of his time in both historical and scientific context.

* *Teach Yourself Evolution*, Morton Jenkins, Teach Yourself Books, Hodder & Stoughton, 1999. Evolution explained in easy terms, useful for the non-scientist.

OUT OF PRINT

If you enjoy wonderfully colourful, illustrated books then try to get hold of these (even if you have to beg, borrow or steal!):

* *The Illustrated Origin of Species*, abridged and introduced by Richard E. Leakey, Faber, 1979.

* *Darwin and the Beagle*, Alan Moorehead, Penguin, 1971.

INDEX

argument by design 54
atheists 61
artificial selection 40
atrophied organs 46
Australia 13,23,42
autobiography 70

barnacles 39
Buffon, Georges-Louis 28

Cambridge University 8, 61
catastrophism 28
Chambers, Robert 31, 58
chromosomes 65, 75
climbing plants 64–65
common plan 45
creationist 26, 42, 46, 76–80
Cuvier, Georges 28

Darwin, Erasmus 1,29
Darwinist 60
Descent of Man 59, 60
DNA 75, 77
domestication 40, 65
Down House 33, 39, 57

early life 1
Edinburgh University 6
education 3
embryological development 45
eugenics 73
evolution 1, 17, 26, 28–32, 35, 47, 58
Expression of Emotions … 67

finches 22, 42

FitzRoy, Robert 14, 15, 23, 58
fossils 19, 27, 41, 44, 51

Galapagos Islands 21, 41, 42, 43
Galton, Francis 72–73
gauchos 18, 33, 43
gemmules 56–57, 73
genetics 30, 75
geology 11, 25, 41, 44, 55

Henslow, John 9, 10, 11, 12, 13, 19, 25, 58
Huxley, Thomas 57–58, 60

illness 32, 33, 35, 57, 60
Industrial Revolution 1
insectivorous plants 68
invertebrates 27

Jenkin, Fleeming 56, 76

Lamarck, Jean Baptiste 29, 38, 58, 73, 77
Lord Kelvin 55
Lyell, Charles 16, 17, 25, 31, 44, 47, 48, 54, 57

Malthus, Thomas 37, 47, 72
marriage and country life 32–34
Marx, Karl 62
Mendel, Gregor 56, 75–76
Mivart, H. St George 55
mutations 77

natural selection 1, 33, 36–38, 55, 73
Neo–Darwinism 73–77
new synthesis 77

orchids 63
Origin of Species 33, 45, 46, 47–59, 60, 61, 63
Owen, Richard 56

Paley, William 53–54
pangenesis 56–57, 65, 73
peppered moth 37
plant experiments 41
progressionism 28
public acceptance 58
public outrage 52–54
punctuated equilibria 78

religion against science 78–80
rheas 43
rudimentary organs 46

seed dispersal 40
selective breeding 38
sexual selection 40, 66, 67
Smiles, Samuel 72
Social Darwinism 72
species 36
Spencer, Herbert 72
survival of the fittest 36, 61, 66

The Beagle 12, 13–24, 26, 33, 41
Tierra del Fuego 13, 14, 20
transmutation 25, 35, 39

Unitarians 2

Wallace, Alfred 47–48
Wedgwood family 2, 14, 32
worms 69–70

SARTRE – A BEGINNER'S GUIDE

George Myerson

Sartre – A Beginner's Guide introduces you to the life and work of this leading novelist, central philosopher and major dramatist. Sartre remains a symbol of the committed writer and thinker, and his existentialism continues to challenge us.

George Myerson's fascinating introduction:

- brings the different phases of Sartre's thought and art to life
- explains the key ideas of Sartre's existentialism using examples from his work
- summarises essential information about characters, plots and arguments in the major works
- puts Sartre in philosophical and historical context.

The facts ... the concepts ... the ideas ...

GANDHI – A BEGINNER'S GUIDE

Genevieve Blais

Gandhi – A Beginner's Guide invites you to take a glimpse into the life of this profound character. Follow his extraordinary quest for morality, justice and spirituality and discover how his strategy of passive resistance achieved social reform. Find out how his influence has now extended far beyond the barriers of a nation.

Genevieve Blais's compelling text investigates:

■ Gandhi's background and the times he lived in
■ Britain's role in the history of India
■ the events leading up to and prior to the Salt March
■ Gandhi's role in the independence of India
■ his assassination and legacy.

The facts … the concepts … the ideas …

DA VINCI –
A BEGINNER'S GUIDE

Ruth Berry

Da Vinci – A Beginner's Guide introduces you to the life and work of a great genius. Leonardo is usually thought of as an artist, but he was also an intellectual giant in the developing field of science and an accomplished musician, architect and engineer. Follow the story of a true genius rich in ideas.

Ruth Berry's lively text investigates:

- Leonardo's background and the times he lived in
- the importance of the Renaissance
- Leonardo's influence on the works of art
- his astounding explorations in science and technology.

The facts … the concepts … the ideas …